Edgar Allan Poe

Edgar Allan Poe in 1845, from a painting by Samuel S. Osgood, now in The New York Historical Society. Courtesy, *The Print and Picture Department, The Free Library of Philadelphia.*

EDGAR ALLAN POE

Irwin Porges

CHILTON BOOKS

A Division of Chilton Company
Publishers
Philadelphia and New York

To my wife CELE
*for her patience, encouragement, and
the hours she has spent in the preparation
of this book*

Copyright © 1963 by
IRWIN PORGES

FIRST EDITION

All Rights Reserved

Published in Philadelphia by Chilton Company,
and simultaneously in Toronto, Canada,
by Ambassador Books, Ltd.

LIBRARY OF CONGRESS CATALOG CARD NUMBER 63-21333

MANUFACTURED IN THE UNITED STATES OF AMERICA
QUINN & BODEN COMPANY, INC., RAHWAY, N. J.

Preface

Thorough research on the part of modern biographers has provided us with a reasonably accurate picture of Poe as a man, and has explained and interpreted the main incidents of his life. Old misconceptions of Poe as a completely irrational individual who lived in his own strange fantasy world—one who *had* to be a half-mad genius to write as he did—are not only false but also obviously absurd. Equally false is the notion that he was a confirmed alcoholic and a drug addict. That he had moments of severe mental depression when he was forced to seek stimulants is evident—and not at all surprising under the circumstances in which he lived. Prolonged periods of poverty and semi-starvation, the permanent illness of his wife, the failure to attain a recognition that he deserved—these were sufficient to disturb *any* man and to produce moments of erratic behavior. But, as a further complication, Poe was not *any* man— he possessed a highly strung nervous system and was a sensitive, creative individual with an artistic temperament. The artist who has a greater capacity to imagine also has a greater capacity to suffer. Certainly Poe was more strongly affected than the average man by his problems and frustrations.

To see this image of Poe more clearly, and to get an insight to his true nature, one has only to open a volume of his collected works and scan the Table of Contents. Here lies a dazzling record of creativity! From his poems, *The Raven, The Conqueror Worm,* the *Sonnet—To Science,* one travels to his mystery and detective stories, *The Gold Bug, The Murders in the Rue Morgue, The Purloined Letter.* And then come the tales, ranging from the horror of *The Fall of the House of Usher* and *The Cask of Amontillado* to the contemplation of natural beauty in *The Domain of Arnheim* and *Landor's Cottage.* As if this weren't enough, we find essays on the most diverse topics—furniture, cryptography, a mechanical chess-player, autography—and literary criticisms of many of the authors of Poe's time.

A man who produced this prodigious number of poems, tales, essays, articles, and literary criticisms must have been one who possessed a faculty for hard work and for sustained periods of clear thinking and reasoning. This collection of writings is the result of a *regular* schedule—of an author who devoted himself to long hours of writing during the major periods of his creative life. It is not the product of *irregularity*, of a man under the *constant* influence of liquor or drugs.

A fuller understanding of Poe can be obtained also through considering the astonishing variety of his works. What kind of man could have written all this? Note, first of all, that much of his writing is not in the popularized area of fantasy and horror, but in fields that demanded logic and sober reflection. A good portion of Poe's time, energy, and ability was directed toward the world of *reality*—of the essay, the article, and literary criticism, and to the scientific deduction of his detective stories. Certainly this output of thoughtful, analytical works presents a picture of an author whose attitudes were generally rational, and whose habits were well disciplined.

His varied writings are, in themselves, concrete evidence of Poe's real nature. Obviously, he was curious and observing, interested in people and events, and had an unusual memory in which he stored information for future use. He drew from a wide background, developed through his extensive readings in fiction, poetry, science, and history. Much of his writing was for magazines and newspapers, and he was required to produce material on assignment and to meet deadlines. All of this indicates that Poe was very much concerned with the problems of everyday living—and not a man who had withdrawn to a private world.

Within this biography are numerous references to his works, and, of course, excerpts from his poems, stories, and essays. The use of these fragments is regrettable; many of Poe's writings deserve a complete presentation. But the excerpts are a necessary compromise, since without them we could neither illustrate the ideas nor demonstrate the force, originality, and beauty of Poe's language.

While the biography does not pretend to be all-inclusive, it is based upon authentic sources, and offers an accurate account of Poe's life. To avoid the possible dullness of a mere detailed summary of events, certain scenes have been dramatized or re-created—but always within the framework of established fact. Beyond this, any biography must stand or fall upon the amount of interest it generates in the reader. I believe that this biography is well designed to bring out Poe's colorful personality and to make his life vivid and exciting. I hope that the most important objective will be achieved—that the reader will be stimulated to obtain Poe's works and read them with a new interest and understanding.

IRWIN PORGES

Contents

I · *The Young Voyager Returns*

THE boy who stood on the deck of the *Martha* watched eagerly as the misty shapes on shore made their magic change into the buildings of a great city. The *Martha* was entering New York Harbor after a voyage of thirty-six days from Liverpool, England. Now she inched her way toward the docks, while eleven-year-old Edgar pressed against the rail, his eyes searching and memorizing every detail of the busy waterfront.

He was a boy with an amazing mind that collected details, experiences, and impressions of people as though he already knew he would have use for them later. The five years spent in England were behind him, but Edgar's school days—especially at ancient Manor House School, with its winding passageways and gloomy, low-ceilinged rooms—would never be forgotten.

Even the happenings on his ocean journeys, from Virginia to England and back, would stay with him forever. Although Edgar was only six when he had first felt the sway of a ship's deck, he had stored away the images of his voyage to England: the bustling docks at the James River where the strong smell of tobacco hung like a cloud over everything; the square-rigged schooners tugging at anchor; and the moment of fear and wonder when he said goodbye to Richmond and the ship moved easily down the river toward Hampton Roads and the open sea.

Now Edgar was returning home. Standing next to him, John Allan, his foster-father, gazed at the enormous city that stretched beyond the harbor.

"You'll find that Richmond and New York are much different," John Allan said. He was a man whose voice could be abrupt and gruff, but toward Edgar he had shown kindness and consideration. Allan and his wife had taken the boy into their home when he was barely two years old. As he turned to watch Edgar, Allan had a smile in his eyes and his hand pressed the boy's arm.

Engrossed in the smooth movement of the ship toward its pier and the sight of the rough, muscular men standing by with their horses and drays to load the cargo, Edgar looked up to nod at the man he had learned to call "Father." Allan's mention of Richmond had started faint memories stirring. The warm southern city was not Edgar's birthplace, but it was the only home that he could remember. His mind began to paint half-forgotten pictures of the white houses, the canals, the broad plantations, and the Negro slaves.

Try as he could, Edgar was unable to bring back clear images of the days before he had lived in Richmond. He had been born in Boston on January 19, 1809; it was there that his mother, Elizabeth Arnold, an actress, was appearing in plays with her husband, David Poe. His parents had been in Boston only six months, before moving on for engagements in New York. Of Edgar's first two years, all that remained in his memory was a strange, confused impression of constantly moving about and of a long period of unhappiness and discomfort.

Some memories of his mother—small glimpses of the large dark eyes or the curly black hair that she passed on to him—flashed through his mind. But there was no recollection of his actor-father who had deserted his mother less than a year after Edgar's birth. Now, at the age of eleven, Edgar was too young to understand his mother's suffering and her ill health, even at the time when his younger sister, Rosalie, had been born. On December 8, 1811, his mother had died of tuberculosis.

The *Martha's* hull was now scraping against the timbers of the pier as Captain Sketchly brought his ship to her resting place after the long voyage. Edgar and Mr. Allan braced themselves against the rail to keep from sliding across the deck; the ship had lurched suddenly before coming to a final stop.

In a cabin below decks, Mrs. Allan, Edgar's foster-mother, with her older sister, Anne, were waiting. With so little to remember of his real mother, Edgar had naturally turned to Mrs. Allan for the love and understanding he needed. They had become very close, ever since that day when Mrs. Allan had come to the home of Edgar's dying mother and seen the two-year-old boy and his sister, Rosalie. The small boy had his mother's delicate features and showed the same charm that had made Mrs. Poe so popular as an actress. The two orphan children were taken into different homes, but they were never to be really separated. The Mackenzies, who lived in Richmond, adopted Rosalie, and Edgar was able to visit his sister often. An older brother, William Henry Poe, born two years before Edgar, was given a home with his grandfather, David Poe, Sr., who lived in Baltimore.

The *Martha* was at anchor now, and the passengers were preparing to disembark. Mr. Allan pressed Edgar's arm. "We must go below and get your mother and Aunt Nancy," he said.

Edgar turned away from the rail. "Is Mother feeling better?" he asked.

"I believe she is still a little shaky," Mr. Allan replied. "We mustn't expect women to be good sailors." He looked at Edgar and smiled. "Even some of our young men have a little trouble with the sea!"

Edgar smiled back. His foster-father was referring to the passage to England five years before. Edgar still remembered how seasick he had been at the beginning of the thirty-four-day voyage.

A short while later, the Allan family went ashore. It was a pleasant, sunny day in mid-July of 1820, and before Edgar stretched the exciting prospect of seeing New York City. Mr. Allan had planned to spend only a few days in New York before leaving for Richmond, but it was not until July 28th that the family was able to make a trip by water again—this time on a steamboat. Mrs. Allan had become so ill that a doctor had to be called. Meanwhile, Edgar spent much time with Mrs. Allan's sister Anne, whom he lovingly called Aunt "Nancy."

His travels abroad, as well as his sea voyages, were over. Never again would Edgar board a ship for an ocean passage. But, to a boy of his sensitivity, the details of these colorful experiences were already being shaped and molded in his mind for his future writing. He had been taken by his foster-father to Mr. Allan's native Scotland and had seen the rich, green Scottish countryside and the crowded industrial cities. Later, the family had gone to London; here Edgar was sent to the Misses Dubourg's boarding school in Chelsea.

The rough Atlantic Ocean, the ships and the sailors that were helpless toys in its grip—these filled Edgar's imagination. His foster-father and his partner, Charles Ellis, were traders who dealt in an amazing variety of items: wheat, teas and coffees, wines and liquors, and of course the much sought-after Virginia tobacco. These were transported to or from other cities and shipped abroad. To Edgar, the ships, in addition to stormy seas and brave seamen, meant the loading of pungent-smelling cargoes on the exciting waterfront of Richmond and at the docks in England.

Years later, in 1838, a strange horror narrative appeared in print. The title page was headed

Beneath it a reader was fascinated by the explanation

Comprising the details of a mutiny and atrocious
butchery on board the American Brig *Grampus,*
on her way to the South Seas, in the month of
June, 1827

Using his childhood experiences to give the story a true flavor
of the sea, Edgar Allan Poe transferred the tale to the South Seas.
He began by saying,

My name is Arthur Gordon Pym. My father was a respectable trader
in sea-stores at Nantucket, where I was born.

The description of Pym's voyage to the South Seas in the whaling
vessel *Grampus* provided Edgar with the opportunity to use all
the sea lore he remembered.

He may have been picturing the docks at Richmond when he
wrote of Pym's sailboat "lying at the old decayed wharf by the
lumber-yard of Pankey & Co., and almost thumping her side out
against the rough logs."

In telling the story, he demonstrated his surprising knowledge
of what he called "proper stowage." The young boy who spent
his time at the office and warehouse of merchant-traders Ellis &
Allan, and saw their cargoes being loaded at the wharves, was a
keen observer:

. . . I must here state that the manner in which this most important
duty had been performed on board the *Grampus* was a most shameless
piece of neglect on the part of Captain Barnard . . . A proper stowage
cannot be accomplished in a careless manner . . . In most kinds of
freight the storage is accomplished by means of a screw. Thus, in a
load of tobacco or flour, the whole is screwed so tightly into the hold of
the vessel that the barrels or hogsheads, upon discharging, are found
to be completely flattened, and take some time to regain their original
shape.

Edgar went on to explain the danger of shipping a cargo of
grain since "it will be liable to shift in a long passage so greatly
as to bring about the most distressing calamities." He had seen
enough of ships to know that they were often tipped up on their
beam-ends. In a ship with poor stowage, Edgar claimed that "the
whole of the cargo tumbles over to the side of the vessel which

lies upon the water," and, as a result, "she is certain to fill in a few seconds and go down." To prevent this disastrous shifting of the grain, he suggested that the cargo should be settled as much as possible before leaving port, and that wooden wedges be driven into the grain.

On August 2nd, with the sights and sounds of New York City behind him, Edgar arrived home in Richmond. To a boy who had been only six when he boarded a ship for England, and had been away for five years, everything looked new and strange. As they traveled by carriage to the home of Charles Ellis, where they planned to live temporarily, he tried to bring back his memories of the city he loved.

How different Richmond now appeared, set in its environment of prosperous Southern life, spacious homes, the river and surrounding woods, and the broad plantations! How different from the London that Edgar could picture so vividly, with the thick, black smoke of its factories darkening the skies—its narrow, dirty streets—its ancient houses.

When Edgar, the Allans, and Aunt Nancy arrived at the Ellis' home on the corner of Franklin and Second Streets, he found nothing in the house itself to stir his imaginative mind. It was an ordinary two-story house, of wood construction, with a gabled roof. But across from the house stretched a landscaped garden which for Edgar became a magical spot. With its tall linden trees, flowers, and vine-covered walls, the garden offered him a place for romantic thoughts and poetic dreams.

He fell naturally back into the friendships he had made in Richmond years before. One, however, would vanish into the misty pleasure-filled days of childhood: he had known lovely little Catherine Poitiaux who had sent her regards to him overseas. She was now forgotten, but Edgar began to associate with other boys and girls of his age. As a young child Edgar had spent much time with Ebenezer Burling; the two boys splashed about in the creeks, and Ebenezer taught Edgar how to swim.

In the fall of 1820, the Allan family moved to a new home on Fifth Street, between Marshall and Clay Streets. Ebenezer lived not too far away, and the two boys enjoyed common interests which drew them together. Sometimes their days were passed in a small sailboat, cruising up and down the James River. But best of all, Edgar loved the evenings when they sat together by the firelight, reading adventure books and talking about journeys to strange, far-off lands.

One evening the boys turned the pages of a book that was a hundred years old and yet so fresh and exciting that they imagined themselves taking part in the perilous happenings.

"What is it called?" Ebenezer had asked, when Edgar began to open the book.

"The Life and Surprizing Adventures of Robinson Crusoe," said Edgar.

They read Defoe's thrilling adventure drama together slowly, line by line, their heads held close, while the flames from the fireplace threw a flickering light over the page.

Edgar never forgot the evenings with *Robinson Crusoe,* and years later described how they "hung breathless and trembling with eagerness over their absorbing—over their entrancing interest."

The boys sat for hours with the pages before them; these were the days that Edgar recalled "when we first found the spirit of wild adventure enkindling within us . . ." Defoe's description of "the terror of the storm," with Robinson Crusoe tumbling into the steep waves after his life-boat overturned, held them gripped in fascination:

The wave that came upon me again, buried me at once twenty or thirty feet deep in its own body, and I could feel myself carried with a mighty force and swiftness towards the shore a very great way; but I held my breath and assisted myself to swim still forward with all my might. I was ready to burst with holding my breath, when, as I felt myself rising up, so to my immediate relief, I found my head and hands shoot out above the surface of the water . . .

As a grown man, with all "those enchanted days of boyhood" gone forever, Edgar wrote, "Alas! the days of desolate islands are no more."

Often Edgar would spend the hours at the Mackenzies', where his sister, Rosalie, lived. Although only a year younger than her brother, Rosalie looked to Edgar for guidance and wanted to be with him at every opportunity. The Mackenzies, who had adopted her, made their place a second home for Edgar, and he became a fast friend of their son Jack's.

In these happy Richmond days, Edgar was popular with all the boys and made many friends. As a natural leader he seemed to draw the others around him. Rob Sully, whose father had appeared on the stage with Edgar's mother and whose uncle was the painter Thomas Sully, was one of his closest chums. Tom Ellis, a little younger than Edgar, would follow him around. Edgar's imaginative mind was balanced by a sturdy body, and he learned quickly how to swim, shoot, and skate. He patiently taught these skills to Tom. In later years, Tom recalled his boyhood with Edgar and wrote:

... I ought to mention that he once saved me from drowning—for having thrown me into the falls headlong, that I might strike out for myself, he presently found it necessary to come to my help, or it would have been too late.

Edgar had been enrolled in Joseph W. Clarke's English and Classical School. The subjects he studied—Latin, Greek, and mathematics—carried on the work he had started in England. But often Edgar remembered the old-fashioned Manor House School at Stoke Newington, in the country near London. In his mind he could see the "large, rambling, cottage-built, and somewhat decayed building in a misty-looking village of England." His memories, which he could never erase, provided the setting for a strange story of two students named William Wilson, both at the Manor House School, which he had published years later. The evil "William Wilson" is involved in a life-and-death struggle with his conscience, or twin "William Wilson."

Making use of his remarkable ability for remembering details and for adding his own imaginative touches to them, Edgar wrote a rich description of the Manor House:

The grounds were extensive, and a high and solid brick wall, topped with a bed of mortar and broken glass, encompassed the whole. This prison-like rampart formed the limit of our domain; beyond it we saw but thrice a week ...

At an angle of the ponderous wall frowned a more ponderous gate. It was riveted and studded with iron bolts, and surmounted with jagged iron spikes. What impressions of deep awe did it inspire!

But the house!—how quaint an old building was this!—to me how veritable a place of enchantment! There was really no end to its windings—to its incomprehensible subdivisions. It was difficult, at any given time, to say with certainty upon which of its two stories one happened to be. From each room to every other there were sure to be found three or four steps either in ascent or descent.

In looking back, and picturing the quaint, ancient building in England where he had attended school, Edgar created the Manor

House in his own original way. He saw it as an enchanted place of mystery, with its secret corners, its twisting corridors, and its pointed Gothic windows. To go with the gloomy atmosphere of his terror-filled story about William Wilson, Edgar invented a new stern character for the Reverend John Bransby, the church pastor:

Of this church the principal of our school was pastor. With how deep a spirit of wonder and perplexity was I wont to regard him from our remote pew in the gallery, as, with step solemn and slow, he ascended the pulpit.

Could this be the same man, Edgar asked, who had stood in the school-room "with sour visage" and with a ruler in his hand, reminding the students of the school regulations? He created Reverend Bransby as a person to be feared:

In a remote and terror-inspiring angle [of the school-room] was a square enclosure of eight or ten feet, comprising the *sanctum,* "during hours" of our principal, the Reverend Dr. Bransby.

Edgar described the *sanctum* as "a solid structure with massy door"; the very sight of this cell-like place was so awe-inspiring to the young students, according to Edgar, that they would never dream of daring to open the huge door when the Reverend was not there. They would sooner have endured the most terrible punishment.

The fearful, mysterious surroundings of old Manor House made a powerful impression on Edgar's mind—so powerful that, twenty years later, his story was to open there and rise in fury to the death-duel of William Wilson and his better self. In the fierce battle at the end, the evil Wilson tells how he wins the duel:

In a few seconds I forced him by sheer strength against the wainscotting [sic], and thus, getting him at mercy, plunged my sword, with brute ferocity, repeatedly through and through his bosom.

Finally, the dying Wilson speaks:

. . . but he spoke no longer in a whisper, and I could have fancied that I myself was speaking while he said:
"*You have conquered, and I yield. Yet henceforward art thou also dead—dead to the World, to Heaven, and to Hope! In me didst thou exist—and in my death, see by this image, which is thine own, how utterly thou hast murdered thyself.*"

In destroying his better self—his conscience—William Wilson had really killed the only part of himself that could have saved him; all hope was now dead and he was dead with it.

To Edgar, the fascinating days in England had given treasured recollections which would reappear in other stories to be written in the future. But, in 1822, he found himself drawn, as if by some inner magnetic force, toward a new and thrilling activity. Edgar had always loved to read poetry and to hear it read aloud. Now the first attempts at creating—at forming the words into rich combinations—came without effort: he had begun to write poetry.

Seated in the office of Ellis & Allan, breathing the pungent odor of the tobacco leaf and gazing dreamily out the window at the workmen on the docks, Edgar would scrawl his poetry across odd pieces of paper. Once he found a torn scrap on which somebody had totaled receipts of $30,000. Edgar turned it upside down and in a small blank space wrote:

—— Poetry by Edgar A. Poe ——

> Last night with many cares and toils oppress'd
> Weary . . . I laid me on a couch to rest

Quite often Edgar would think of a pretty girl he particularly liked and write a poem about her. But, even at this early period, he was fascinated by thoughts of horror and death. He found a ragged strip of paper on the desk in the Ellis & Allan office and composed a strange poem of gloom:

> Flow softly—gently—vital stream;
>   Ye crimson life drops, stay;
> Indulge me with this pleasing dream
>   Thro' an eternal day
>
> See—see—my soul, her agony!
> See how her eyeballs glare!
> Those shrieks delightful harmony,
> Proclaim her deep despair.
>
> Rise—rise—infernal spirits, rise
> Swift dart acrop her brain
> Thou Horror with blood chilling cries
> lead on thy hidious train
>
> O, feast my soul revenge is sweet
>   Louisa, take my scorn;—
> Curs'd was the hour that saw us meet
> the hour when we were born.

In his odd imagination, the thirteen-year-old Edgar seemed to enjoy the horrifying images he painted. His words now were the same frightening ones he would paint later—"eyeballs glare," "shrieks," "blood chilling cries"—these weird things he loved to write about!

But at home he often turned to romantic ideas. Coming into his room, Mrs. Allan would stand silently behind him as he wrote, watching the lines of poetry appear.

"What is it this time?" she would ask, putting a hand on his shoulder. "Another girl?"

Edgar reddened, embarrassed by the gay, joking laughter in his foster-mother's voice. He was very fond of her and would show her his poems as soon as they were written.

She felt that Edgar had unusual ability and was quite proud of him. "You must read it aloud," she would tell him, whenever he had completed a new poem. "I'd like to hear it."

In the months that passed, Edgar began to take an interest in the young ladies who were attending a fashionable boarding school in Richmond. The school was conducted by Jane Mackenzie, whose sister-in-law, Mrs. William Mackenzie, had made a place for Rosalie Poe, Edgar's little sister. Edgar not only wrote poems to the girls who caught his fancy, but also displayed surprising skill in drawing sketches of them. With Rosalie eager to do whatever he asked, Edgar had no trouble in getting her to be his messenger—she joined in the romantic game with glee and contrived to pass her brother's poems and sketches secretly to certain young ladies at the school.

At the school which he attended, Edgar developed a strong liking for the headmaster. Joseph Clarke was an impulsive Irishman with a quick temper; on occasion he spoke sharply to the students, but he could also be considerate and understanding.

One day Clarke looked up from his desk in surprise to discover John Allan standing there. "Why, Mr. Allan!" he said, in his gruff voice. "We're delighted to have you visit us." He had already noted the thick bundle of paper that Allan carried under his arm.

John Allan smiled and nodded. "The reason I'm here," he said, "is because I want your opinion about something. As you probably know, Edgar has taken to writing poetry." His voice, normally without emotion, now had a touch of pride.

"Yes," said Clarke. His eyes had an amused glint. He knew

about Edgar's romantic poetry and his interest in the town's young ladies.

"He may have some ability in writing," Allan said. "I wonder if you would look at them?"

Clarke took the roll of papers. He was surprised at its thickness. He opened it and leafed through the pages. "I never imagined Edgar had written so many poems," he said.

"I'll leave them with you," Allan told him. He turned to go, and hesitated. "My wife and I thought they might be suitable for publication. Please let me know."

After John Allan had left, Clarke sat for a while thinking about Edgar. He had been pleased that a young boy should have so unusual an interest. At the school he rarely encountered students with creative ability, especially in the field of poetry. He turned the pages and read parts of the poems.

He was impressed by the boy's use of colorful words and his excellent vocabulary. However, he didn't think that the poems showed enough originality; many of the phrases resembled those that had been used often in the English poems of the day.

Still, Clarke was an astute enough man to realize that Edgar was far above the average boy in many ways. He seemed to combine the playfulness of a young boy with the maturity of an adult. Edgar liked sports, took part in all the games with the other students, was popular, and yet managed to appear as one apart from them.

Clarke thought of the boy's unusual character: remarkable self-respect without haughtiness; strictly just and correct in his behavior toward the other students; enthusiastic about everything he tried; very stubborn in an argument when his opinion was questioned, and unyielding unless he was convinced he was wrong. Added to this was the fact that Edgar seemed to learn quickly without putting in long hours of study.

"A strongly individualistic boy," Clarke murmured to himself. As he pictured Edgar's actions, he decided that two qualities stood out above all: his imaginative ability in writing, and his sensitive and tender heart which would never allow him to turn down a friend who needed help.

For Edgar the years 1822–1823 passed pleasantly in Richmond. Life seemed normal, with his school work, his friends, and his sister, Rosalie. At home he had the love and understanding of his foster-mother and his Aunt Nancy. But often he wished that Mr.

Allan would be warmer in his attitude toward him. Then Edgar might be able to forget a disturbing thought that kept returning—the reminder that he had no real parents.

Edgar, extremely sensitive, had now begun to feel that, for some unexplainable reason, he was losing Mr. Allan's affection. The man whom he had always called Father—in fact, the only father he had ever known—was not one to show affection openly. He was a stern man whose small, sharp eyes, hooked nose, and shaggy eyebrows gave his face a disapproving, demanding look. Still, Edgar knew that in the past Mr. Allan had been kind to him on many occasions. He could recall how Mr. Allan had talked to him, shown interest in his school work, and been proud of his achievements.

Now Edgar noticed that his foster-father was continually curt and often angry, not only with him but also with other members of the household. The friends who visited Edgar at home were aware of Mr. Allan's short temper and his impatience. The home had become an uncomfortable, gloomy place; quarrels were frequent, and Mr. Allan rarely said an affectionate word to the boy. Edgar hesitated to invite his friends any more, and began instead to pass the hours at the Mackenzie home with his chum, Jack, and his sister, Rosalie.

Knowing little about Mr. Allan's business affairs, Edgar could not understand that one reason for his foster-father's behavior was the serious financial condition of the firm of Ellis & Allan. The hope had been to set up a branch of the company in England, but Mr. Allan's plans had failed. There had been a depression; business was bad everywhere and he lost much money. Actually, Mr. Allan's rich uncle, William Galt, had backed the firm, and both he and Charles Ellis were upset over the losses. In 1822, with Ellis & Allan bankrupt, Edgar's foster-father was on the verge of losing all his property. Fortunately, the wealthy Mr. Galt persuaded his creditors not to foreclose, and the company was temporarily saved.

2 · To Helen: *A First Touch of Tragedy*

THE association between Joseph Clarke, headmaster at the English and Classical School, and Edgar had developed into more than that of a teacher and a bright student. In their months together, common liking and respect had deepened into a warm attachment. Clarke admired Edgar both personally and for his ability as a student; he was especially pleased that he had never had occasion to speak a harsh word to the boy. With the headmaster's constant help, Edgar had made excellent progress in Latin. Wanting very much to show his appreciation, in 1822 he and his friend, Nat Howard, wrote letters to Clarke. Both were in Latin, but Edgar's complimented Joseph Clarke in original verses. The headmaster never forgot this.

In the fall of 1823, Edgar heard news which made him despondent. Joseph Clarke had decided to return to his home in Baltimore; his school was to be taken over by a new owner. At the farewell ceremony, Edgar was given permission to address the audience of parents and students. He arose, and in his clear, precise voice recited an English ode which he had written and dedicated to Clarke. Many of those gathered there were astonished at the fourteen-year-old boy's ability to create such poetry.

For his new schoolmaster, William Burke, Edgar never developed a strong affection. Still, he remained a good student and became a leader among a group of boys who looked up to him because of his many accomplishments. With Rob Sully, Richard Ambler, and Creed Thomas, he organized a boys' drama group called the Thespian Society. Performances were given in an old wooden building on Sixth and Marshall Streets; as many as forty or fifty people would pay a penny to watch the amateur actors.

But the boy who displayed a variety of talent that made others respect him was not always in a serious mood. Edgar loved practical jokes. During a Christmas evening at home, with Tom Ellis and his sister Jane present, Edgar came into the room carrying a toy snake—a long, slim, shiny one made in sections and fastened together by wires. Tom watched while Edgar waved it in front of

Jane, making it wriggle and dart about as though it were alive. The young girl was frightened and screamed. Later, Tom became annoyed with Edgar as he continued poking the snake into Jane's face.

Edgar's fondness for pranks was so great that he didn't hesitate to play them upon adults. Tom Ellis never forgot the sudden appearance of a "ghost" at a meeting of the Gentlemen's Whist Club. The players were "in truth stirred to a commotion." Years later Tom recalled,

General Winfield Scott, one of the invited guests, with the resolution and promptness of an old soldier, sprang forward as if he was leading a charge in Lundy's Lane. Dr. Phillip Thornton, of Rappahannock, another guest, was, however, nearer to the door and quicker than he. Presently the ghost, finding himself closely pressed, began to retreat, backing around the room, yet keeping his face to the foe, and as the Doctor was reaching out and trying to seize the ghost's nose with the view to twitch it off, the ghost was "larruping" him over the shoulder with the long cane which he carried in one hand, while with the other hand he was struggling to keep from being tripped by the sheet which enveloped his body. When finally forced to surrender and the mask was taken from the face, Edgar laughed as heartily as ever a ghost did before.

Amid all the suffering and trouble of his later life, Edgar never lost his glee over an ingenious prank. As a successful writer he found a new form for his practical jokes: he astounded and fooled the public in his famous literary hoaxes—*The Unparalleled Adventures of One Hans Pfaall,* who took a journey to the moon, and the celebrated *Balloon-Hoax,* in which a "flying machine," actually a "steering balloon" with a propeller, crossed the Atlantic in three days!

Beyond all these amazing abilities and interests, Edgar had one which his young friends valued most of all. He was the best athlete of the group. He had a natural love of sports and was especially strong in swimming, running, and even boxing.

One day a large crowd of students and some of their parents gathered at the James River bank near Ludlow's Wharf.

"Do you think he'll really do it?" one boy asked.

"Of course he will," said Robert Cabell, one of Edgar's friends.

Nearby, Rob Sully, a thin, frail boy, spoke up. "Edgar is the best swimmer in town," he said. "And he always does what he promises." Sully, Edgar's closest friend, was always his staunchest supporter. A sensitive, artistic boy, Sully felt a deep affection and gratitude toward Edgar, who had encouraged him in many ways and had helped him in school with his Latin and mathematics.

"There he comes!" somebody shouted, and the students turned to watch Edgar as he walked toward the wharf. The word had spread quickly that Edgar had boasted of his intention to swim down the James River from Richmond to Warwick Bar. This was the scheduled day.

Robert Mayo ran forward to meet Edgar. "I'm going to swim it with you," he said, excitedly.

Nearby, Rob Sully clutched Edgar's hand. "I *told* them you'd keep your promise," he said.

Edgar smiled. "I'm ready," he told his friend.

He walked onto the wharf and looked down into the water. Fastened to the wharf was a rowboat, and Edgar was surprised to see his schoolmaster, William Burke, seated in the boat.

Burke looked up at him. "I'll be paddling along," he said. His eyes flashed an amused gleam. "You might want company—if your strength gives out."

Edgar nodded and looked up at the sky. It was a hot June day, without even a hint of a breeze; overhead the sun was a blazing ball of fire and he could feel the warmth of its rays on his arms and shoulders. Edgar was very proud of his swimming ability: he was confident that he could swim the distance of six miles down the James.

He slipped over the edge of the wharf and dropped into the water. Behind him he heard a splash and twisted his neck to see Robert Mayo treading water, ready to follow.

As Edgar plunged ahead he felt the drag of the tide; it was stronger than he had anticipated. The water was surprisingly warm and it seemed to reflect the intense, uncomfortable glare of the sun which almost blinded him.

On the muddy bank, Robert Cabell and young Rob Stanard followed gleefully. They and several other students planned to accompany Edgar as far as he went, by walking along the river's edge. A curious crowd lined the river bank, watching Edgar's arms rise and fall. William Burke stroked his oars slowly, keeping his boat well behind, and soon other boats were shoved into the water and students clambered in, to hoot and cry and join the procession.

Edgar, fresh and filled with energy, swam with ease. He was surprised at the strong tide and knew that it would make his six-mile swim more difficult. After a while the sun began to burn his face and back; he could feel sharp tingling pains on his exposed skin. But he knew he hadn't even begun to tire; he still stroked smoothly, with little effort. In the distance he could spy Tree Hill, to him a half-way marker. Splashing sounds nearby reminded him that Robert Mayo was still swimming.

He turned his head around and grinned. "How are you doing?" he asked.

The other boy shook his head. He was puffing hard and his body seemed stiff and strained. "Don't know," he gasped. "Try to go on . . . Getting tired . . ."

"Good luck," said Edgar, as he pulled ahead. Mayo began falling farther and farther behind.

Minutes later, Tree Hill loomed above the river. "Three miles down, three to go," Edgar murmured as he looked up. He could feel some tiredness gripping his muscles now, but he wasn't worried. Deep inside he knew that there was sufficient reserve strength. He was unaware that Robert Mayo had given up at Tree Hill and been helped into one of the boats.

The sun's rays were now scorchingly hot, and the skin on his face and neck seemed alive with pain. But the boy stroked doggedly on, still fighting the tide. He was barely conscious of the shouts and calls from the river bank. A heaviness was beginning to grip his legs and arms; his breathing became heavier, but he would not allow his pace to slow. After a while he could glimpse the shadowy outline of Warwick Bar. It was still a long distance away, but the sight of it heartened him.

Meanwhile, joined by a group of towns-people, Edgar's friends were running along the muddy bank. Rob Stanard had grown more and more excited as Edgar passed the half-way mark. He ran down the bank near the water's edge crying, "Keep it up, Edgar! Keep it up!" When Edgar drew near to Warwick Bar, Rob, hardly aware of what he was doing, slid about in the shallow water while he kept calling, "You're almost there! Just a little farther!" Rob's shoes and pants were soaking wet and he was splattered with mud from head to foot.

Edgar was now within a few hundred yards of the Bar and could see the crowd waiting for him. He was tired and his back felt raw and inflamed, but he knew that he would make his six-mile goal with energy to spare. Minutes later, as the crowd shouted and cheered, he swam up to the Bar and was helped out of the water by his friends.

Edgar smiled at Rob Stanard who had seized his hand and was sputtering words of congratulation. Nearby, Edgar heard Robert Mayo call his name. He turned as Mayo came over to grab his arm and cry, "You made it, Edgar—a six-mile swim!" Mayo shook his head ruefully. "I couldn't get any farther than Tree Hill."

"I'm sorry," said Edgar. "Maybe you can try it again some time. The sun was terribly hot." He rubbed his fingers over his neck and winced at the pain.

"You're blistered," said Mayo. "Even on your face."

Edgar pressed the sorest spots carefully and found that blisters had formed on his face, neck, and back. But he was so elated over his successful swim that he hardly noticed the soreness. "Let's walk back to town," he told Mayo and Stanard.

The headmaster, William Burke, had come over to congratulate him and shake his hand. "You still have energy enough to walk back?" Burke asked in surprise.

"Of course," said Edgar. "I'm not very tired." He and his friends set off to walk along the river bank, chatting happily and joking all the way back to town.

As the months went by, Edgar began spending more and more of his leisure time away from home. The old friendly relationship with Mr. Allan that he remembered so well seemed to be vanishing. The man he tried to think of as his father was displeased with him often. Made uncomfortable by the bickering and tension at home, Edgar visited with Rob Stanard, Jack Mackenzie, and other friends. In Mrs. Allan and his Aunt Nancy he still found a warm understanding; he turned to them naturally when he was in trouble or needed advice.

Mr. Allan's business affairs had not improved; in fact, he remained in business only because of the aid given by his wealthy uncle, William Galt. In 1824, Charles Ellis and John Allan finally agreed to dissolve their firm and operate separately. At the same time, the Allan family moved to a house on the corner of Fourteenth Street and Tobacco Alley in Richmond; the house was owned by William Galt.

One afternoon, with school out, Edgar and Rob Stanard were walking slowly along the street. To Rob, a younger boy, Edgar was a natural leader—someone he had always admired. "Why don't you come to my house for a while?" Rob asked.

Edgar hesitated. For the past several days his father had been annoyed because he believed that Edgar was spending too much time with his friends. "I don't know," said Edgar. "I guess I'd better not."

"But you promised," Rob protested. "You've never been at my place."

Edgar was very fond of Rob and didn't want to hurt his feelings. "All right," he said. "Just for a little while."

On Ninth Street across from Capital Square, Rob stopped to point. "That's my house there," he said. "The one with the large garden."

When they had climbed the stairs and entered the house, Rob said, "I want you to meet my mother. I told her about you."

They hadn't heard the quiet footsteps and didn't know that someone had entered the room until a woman's laughing voice, soft and musical, caught their attention: "And *I* want to meet Edgar! I've heard so much about him!"

Edgar turned to stare at the woman who stood facing him. It was a moment and a memory that would stay with him for the rest of his life. He barely heard Rob say proudly, "This is my mother," and somehow managed to stutter, "How do you do, Mrs. Stanard."

Mrs. Stanard took the hand the boy held out and smiled at him. "Welcome to our home," she said. "Rob has talked about you so often that I feel I already know you!"

Edgar thought he had never seen a woman so beautiful. But his sensitive mind reached out, almost instantly, for something else that he could feel in her—something beneath the lovely face and the warm smile. In some magical way, Edgar understood that, with Mrs. Jane Stith Stanard, he would find the closeness and the sympathy that he had never possessed before. In that moment the two were drawn together by some hidden force; for Edgar, at least, the attachment was one of the spirit and the soul, so deep that it would be a life inspiration.

In the days that followed, he came to visit her whenever he was troubled by happenings at home. She soothed and comforted him, and, in additon, became the main audience for his poetry. In writing about her, Edgar said that she had been the "first, purely ideal love" of his soul. As a boy of fifteen years, the love he felt for the thirty-one-year-old Mrs. Stanard was a worshiping, idealistic one; for a boy who would forever be a lover of beauty and virtue, it was the kind of love that was bound to reappear in years to come. He would always worship beauty in every form.

The Stanards' garden became Edgar's favorite spot. Here he, Rob, and Mrs. Stanard would sit on sunny days. "Read one of your poems," she would say.

Edgar needed no further encouragement to read to her. The poem was usually one of his latest ones. He read in a calm, confident voice, his eyes lifting every now and then to watch for a change of expression. When her face lit up with enjoyment, he was thrilled. From Mrs. Stanard he gained both appreciation and suggestions for improving his poetry.

But during these meetings, always keenly alert to people's attitudes, Edgar began to notice that Mrs. Stanard was changing in a disturbing way. Much of her gayety had vanished; she seemed moody and depressed. Often, when he read to her, he realized that she was not listening. At times her face would twist and contort, as though she were in pain.

"There's something wrong with your mother," Edgar told Rob.

Rob nodded, his eyes dark with worry. "Yes," he said. "She isn't feeling well."

"What does the doctor say?" Edgar asked. "Is it something serious?"

"I'm not certain," Rob said. He spoke in a low tone and seemed deeply troubled. "I think they're hiding the truth from me. I'm afraid—" His voice trailed away.

"Afraid of what?" Edgar demanded quickly. He met Rob's despondent glance while a sudden chill gripped him. No further words were necessary. He stood dazed, unwilling to believe that the woman he worshiped was seriously ill. "It can't be—it mustn't be—" The words ran through his mind.

The next day he sat with Rob, hoping that Mrs. Stanard would come into the room. When she did arrive, Edgar was distressed by the further change in her manner and her appearance. She barely spoke to him. When she did talk, her words seemed disconnected; she started to tell the boys something and then shifted abruptly to a new subject. She laughed every now and then in a high-pitched voice.

Although Edgar felt that nothing could destroy her beauty, he realized sadly that her face was much thinner and that there were dark hollows under her eyes. She tugged nervously at her hair, and brushed the uncombed strands away from her face.

Edgar saw her irregularly after that. At times she seemed almost normal, chatting with him and listening to his poems. But now he watched her in dread. From Rob he had learned the terrible nature of her illness: Mrs. Stanard was going insane.

As she moved deeper into the agony of her mental disorder, Mrs. Stanard turned critically ill. Edgar knew that she was dying. He saw her for a short time in the last period of her suffering. On April 28, 1824, Mrs. Stanard died. She was buried in the family plot in Shockoe Cemetery.

For Edgar, days of brooding and anguish followed. In the death of Jane Stanard he had lost his dearest friend and the one who had given him the help and the encouragement he so desperately needed. But, as an imaginative boy of fifteen, the greatest, unforgettable tragedy was the loss of the beautiful woman he worshiped—his first ideal love.

Later, the story arose that a young boy went each night to the cemetery where he stood weeping over Mrs. Stanard's grave. Was it really so? A deeply sensitive boy like Edgar might be driven to haunt the grave of the woman he loved, for her death had a profound effect upon him. For months afterward he appeared like one drifting hopelessly in an unreal world.

Jack Mackenzie, who had noticed his disturbed behavior, spoke to Edgar about it. "You seem to be far off in your own thoughts," he told Edgar, "—as though you were buried in gloom."

Edgar was silent for a moment. For a number of nights he had been sleeping badly, troubled by frightening nightmares. His dreams were always the same: he would find himself lost in blackness and with unknown menacing creatures moving closer and closer until he could hear them breathing. All about him was the atmosphere of the dead and of damp, moldy graves. At times he lay half-awake, peering into his dark room and trying to break through the web of the dream that held him.

"It's the most horrible thing you can imagine," he said, in describing his dreams to Jack. "I feel an ice-cold hand laid upon my face in a pitch-dark room when I'm alone at night; or I awaken in semi-darkness and see an evil face gazing close into mine." He shuddered. "It becomes unbearable and I keep my head under the bed-covering until I'm nearly suffocated."

Jack watched Edgar worriedly. "It's best not to think about such things," he said.

For Edgar, death, terror, and evil things were always to be close. But soon he succeeded in throwing off the gloom that had gripped him. Jane Stanard became a beautiful dream and memory. He thought of her as possessing the kind of perfect Greek beauty that he had always admired. In school he had been studying Greek and Roman literature. It seemed to him that the works of Homer and the story of Helen of Troy were the most fascinating writings he had ever read. From the woman whose beauty caused the Trojan War he took his favorite name, and Mrs. Stanard became to him that lovely, deathless woman. For some time Edgar had known that he must write a poem dedicated to her. The lines were begun now, and shaped and polished until he felt that they were perfect. To his ideal "Helen," a boy of fifteen found the words telling of her perfection, but it was not until 1831 that the words were molded the way Edgar wanted them and the poem appeared in print:

> Helen, thy beauty is to me
> Like those Nicean barks of yore,
> That gently, o'er a perfumed sea,
> The weary, way-worn wanderer bore
> To his own native shore.
>
> On desperate seas long wont to roam,
> Thy hyacinth hair, thy classic face,
> Thy Naiad airs have brought me home
> To the glory that was Greece,
> And the grandeur that was Rome.
>
> Lo! in yon brilliant window-niche
> How statue-like I see thee stand,
> The agate lamp within thy hand!
> Ah, Psyche, from the regions which
> Are Holy-Land!

3 · *You Were All to Me, Love*

CREATING the beauty of Jane Stanard in his poetry helped Edgar overcome the sadness that filled his mind. The events of daily life, his schooling and visits with his friends—all kept him occupied. At home, his relations with his father were not improving. Although Mr. Allan's financial troubles may have been responsible for his impatient attitude, it was still difficult to understand why he should act so harshly toward Edgar. The days at home were bearable only because of the warm sympathy Edgar received from Mrs. Allan, whom he loved very much, and from his Aunt Nancy. More and more, when not with Jack Mackenzie, Ebenezer Burling, or his other friends, Edgar began withdrawing from the family circle to sit alone in his room. As a young boy he had been genuinely fond of John Allan; now an antagonism toward his father was growing. One disturbing fact was becoming clearer to him each day: he did not really belong in the Allan family, for John Allan had never officially adopted him. He must look upon his life there as only temporary.

In the fall of 1824, an exciting event was to take place in Richmond: the Marquis de La Fayette was scheduled to visit the city. At school Edgar had always liked military display—the marching, the drilling, and especially the colorful uniforms. The plans for a huge military procession to greet La Fayette had given the younger boys an idea: why not form a company of junior volunteers to take part in the celebration of the Marquis's visit?

The boys got together to choose their leaders. "John Lyle for Captain!" somebody shouted. In the vote that followed, Lyle was elected. Then several of the boys looked at Edgar. "We need a lieutenant," a boy said. "Edgar Allan Poe for lieutenant!" several cried at once.

Edgar flushed happily, not only at the prospect of receiving the honor, but also at the thought that he was liked by the others. When the vote came in, it was unanimous for Edgar as lieutenant of the Richmond Junior Volunteers.

"What about arms?" someone asked. "We must have them if we're to march in the parade."

"We must request permission to take whatever we need from the armory," said Edgar.

"Yes," said "Captain" John Lyle—"Edgar and I will arrange everything."

On Tuesday afternoon, October 26, 1824, La Fayette entered Richmond. Although it was raining, he was greeted by large crowds. The next day the formal parade and ceremony took place. Edgar, in his lieutenant's uniform, with a gleaming sword fastened to his side, stood guard and marched in the parade. He was especially thrilled because the Marquis remembered Edgar's grandfather, David Poe, who had been called "General" Poe because he had fought so gallantly with the American revolutionary army against the British.

Edgar found his military experience so exciting that he remained as lieutenant of the Richmond Junior Volunteers after La Fayette had left the city. Perhaps, above all, he enjoyed the feeling of independence and authority this gave him.

At an earlier time, Edgar had shown a natural interest in girls of his own age and had written romantic poems for them. Now, as a boy of fifteen, he began to take notice of a lovely young girl whose home was opposite his. Her name was Sarah Elmira Royster; she was about Edgar's age, and for him her dark eyes and gleaming black hair, in combination with her sweetness and gayety, were irresistible.

The two began to spend their spare hours together. They went for long walks or for trips to the countryside near Richmond. Sometimes they sat in the garden near Charles Ellis' home, where Edgar had lived when he first returned to Richmond. Here, in the seclusion offered by the linden trees and the old brick walls, Elmira and Edgar sat and talked and dreamed of the future. To Edgar it seemed that all his cares and worries had vanished beyond the walls and that he was alone with "Myra" in a magic, enchanted garden.

One day Edgar entered the house to hear his mother call to him. He walked into his mother's room to find her sitting there with his Aunt Nancy. Noting the serious expressions on their faces, he asked, "Is anything wrong?"

"It's about your father's uncle—Mr. Galt," his mother said. "He died last night."

"I'm sorry," said Edgar. He knew that the wealthy Mr. Galt had been very generous with his father and had helped him through his business troubles. He also knew that Mr. Galt was quite old and that his death had been expected.

"Yes," said Aunt Nancy, "we are all very sorry." She hesitated.

"But there is something else. You've heard about Mr. Galt's will. You know that he has a great deal of money. This will mean a lot to your father. Mr. Galt has left him a large sum."

Edgar was quite excited at the news. He knew that Mr. Galt was worth more than $500,000. Now all the family's money worries were over. But, as he walked out of the room with his Aunt Nancy, he was conscious of another worry that had been with him for the past few weeks. His mother, Frances Allan, had never been a strong woman. In England and on board the ship, Edgar could recall that she had had periods of illness. Watching her at home, he noticed that she was losing weight and seemed pale and tired most of the time. The doctor visited her regularly.

"Can anything be done about Mother?" he asked his Aunt Nancy.

She pressed Edgar's hand. "I hope she'll be all right. Don't you worry about it."

The memory of Jane Stanard's suffering and death returned to pain him. Now that Mr. Galt was gone, it seemed to Edgar that death was a dreadful apparition that always hovered near, waiting to seize the people he loved. He was chilled by the fear that his mother might be the next one on death's list.

By the spring of 1825, with the probate of William Galt's will, John Allan became a wealthy man. Soon the excited Edgar noticed many bustling preparations: his father had bought a large home on the corner of Main and Fifth Streets and they must be ready to move at once. When they arrived at the new home, Edgar was delighted. John Allan intended now to take his place in the best Richmond society; the house he had selected was the most spacious Edgar had ever seen. It had a reception or tea room, a large dining room, and, on the second floor, an elaborate parlor or ballroom for special affairs. At the end of the hall on the second floor was Edgar's room, well fitted out with a table, a wardrobe, bookcases, and a cosy lounge. Edgar was supplied with new clothes in the latest fashion.

Edgar's room, at the northeast corner of the house, gave him a view of the James River. He could walk out onto the upstairs porch and gaze at the city that spread out before him. But best of all, Edgar loved to use the telescope that his father had brought from England. He would invite his friends to come out on the porch with him and they would spend hours gazing at the stars and the planets. At this time, Edgar began to read every book he could find on the subject of astronomy; he collected an amazing amount of information. To him the moon was especially fascinating, and he never tired of reading about it and building fanciful stories in his mind about the pale night orb.

Later, in *The Unparalleled Adventures of One Hans Pfaall,* Edgar wrote of an imaginary journey to the moon, using all his knowledge of astronomy in this story, and in the *Balloon-Hoax.* Hans Pfaall, in his strange adventures, disappears from Rotterdam and nothing is heard from him for five years. Edgar wrote a tongue-in-cheek story, enjoying the chance to poke fun at other accounts of trips to the moon and to use comical Dutch-sounding names.

Like Washington Irving, who loved to fill his humorous tales with collections of such Dutch names as the Knickerbockers, the Van Bummels, Van Warts, Van Winkles, and Onderdonks, Edgar chose names that would bring smiles to his readers' faces. As his story opens, a large crowd is waiting in the great square of the Exchange of the city of Rotterdam. They are staring upward toward a strange descending object. In the crowd is the burgomaster Mynheer Superbus Von Underduk and President Rubadub of the College of Astronomy. As the balloon drops toward the earth, the astounded Dutch citizens see that it is made entirely of dirty newspapers, in shape "being little or nothing better than a huge fool's-cap turned upside down."

The crowd gazed at the balloon's only occupant—a little man only two feet high. Edgar jokingly offered his description of a moon man:

The body of the little man was more than proportionately broad, giving to his entire figure a rotundity highly absurd. . . . His hands were enormously large. His hair was gray, and collected in a queue behind. His nose was prodigiously long, crooked and inflammatory; his eyes full, brilliant and acute; his chin and cheeks, although wrinkled with age, were broad, puffy, and double; but of ears of any kind there was not a semblance to be discovered upon any portion of his head.

Rotterdam's curious citizens waited impatiently for the balloon to drop to earth, but its descent had been stopped at about one hundred feet in altitude. The moon man produced a large morocco pocket-book from which he took "a huge letter sealed with red sealing-wax and tied carefully with red tape." He let it fall "precisely at the feet of the burgomaster, Superbus Von Underduk."

Then the moon man threw out a half-dozen bags of ballast. They tumbled "upon the back of the burgomaster, and rolled him over and over no less than half a dozen times, in the face of every individual in Rotterdam."

The huge letter contains a message from Hans Pfaall, who explains that he is very anxious to return from the moon to his family. Unfortunately, when he took off in his balloon five years before, the fierce explosion had caused the death of three of his creditors whom he had deceived into helping him launch the balloon. Hans now asks for a pardon in return for all the valuable information about the moon he can offer the city of Rotterdam.

As the balloon becomes a speck in the sky, Professor Rubadub suggests that "the pardon would be of little use, as no one but a man of the moon would undertake a voyage to so vast a distance."

Edgar's story of Hans Pfaall was a delightful spoof; still, he tried to make his details of the voyage as scientifically accurate as possible. At the end of the story, in commenting about other writers of "moon" stories, he said:

> The writers seem, in each instance, to be utterly uninformed in respect to astronomy. In "Hans Pfaall" the design is original, inasmuch as regards an attempt at *verisimilitude,* in the application of scientific principles (so far as the whimsical nature of the subject would permit), to the actual passage between the earth and the moon.

The year 1825 found sixteen-year-old Edgar in a comfortable situation, now that John Allan had become wealthy. He had everything he needed: his well-furnished room, his telescope, and the company of his many friends. Added to this was his romance with Elmira Royster; she had become dearer to him as each day passed.

But, because of other happenings at home, Edgar could not feel really secure. Mr. Allan's constant criticism of his behavior led Edgar to withdraw often to the privacy of his room. The close affection he shared with Mrs. Allan and Aunt Nancy gave him some reassurance. Still, although Edgar could not realize it, the love that his mother showed toward him made John Allan jealous and unhappy.

"You have a surprise visitor," Aunt Nancy told him one afternoon. "Someone's waiting for you in the tea room."

When Edgar walked into the room and saw the boy in a naval uniform he gave a cry of pleasure. "Henry!" he said.

William Henry Poe, his older brother, smiled and grabbed his hand. "I told you I would come," he said.

Edgar had been corresponding with his brother for years, ever since Henry had lived in Baltimore with their grandparents. Edgar's grandfather, the famous General David Poe, had died in 1816, leaving Grandma Eliza and Henry without financial support.

"Tell me all about the sea," said Edgar. He admired his brother and now thought wistfully that a life at sea would be very exciting.

They talked for some time, with Henry telling Edgar about his experiences in the merchant marine and the foreign lands he had seen. The eighteen-year-old Henry was not a strong boy; he was thin and slight and had little of Edgar's athletic ability. But, like Edgar, he possessed the creative streak that both may have inherited from Elizabeth Arnold Poe, their actress-mother, and her actor-husband David Poe. Henry was also writing poetry and was eager to read Edgar's poems.

The two boys went up to Edgar's room, where Henry gazed enviously at the luxurious furniture; he was taken out on the porch and shown Edgar's telescope.

"Tell me," Henry said, linking his arm into Edgar's, "What about the girls? I'll bet they flock around you!"

Edgar reddened. "There's just one," he said. "Myra—her name's Elmira Royster."

"Sounds serious," said Henry, grinning. "Can I meet her?"

"I thought we might go over to her house later," said Edgar.

The boys stopped to see Ebenezer Burling, whom Henry had known for some time; then the three went on to Elmira's house.

"This is my brother, Henry," Edgar told Elmira. "He's in on a short visit before returning to sea."

Elmira remembered Edgar's speaking about Henry; Ebenezer had been at her house a number of times. She thought Ebenezer interesting but did not approve of his behavior and his influence on Edgar. To her, Ebenezer seemed to lead an irregular, dissipated life.

After they had chatted for a while, Henry said, "How about some music?" He had noticed the piano in one corner of the room. "I've heard from Edgar that you play very well."

Elmira flushed. "Edgar is exaggerating," she said. "But if he's willing to play the flute, I'll accompany him on the piano."

Edgar had always been interested in music. Whenever he and Myra got together she would play, and Edgar would join her in singing or try solos on the flute.

Now the time passed quickly as Myra sat down at the piano, Edgar chimed in with the flute, and they all sang. The hours spent with his brother Henry seemed also to slip away quickly and it was with sadness that they finally had to say goodbye.

"I'll try to see you again soon," said Henry. "And I'll send you some poems I've been working on."

Edgar nodded, suddenly touched by gloom and dejection. Once his brother would leave, he felt he would have nobody who was really close to him. Thoughts of the tension at home with his father flooded through his mind. He fought to control the loneliness that seized him. He gripped his brother's hand. "I'd like to run away to sea!" he exclaimed.

Henry looked at him in amazement. "Why would you want to do that? You have it so comfortable here."

Edgar remained silent, his face turned away. Henry examined him with concern. "Things aren't too bad, are they?" he asked. Henry was aware of the situation between Edgar and his father.

"No, they aren't too bad," Edgar replied slowly. He smiled at his brother. "You're the one who's really lucky. To be able to go to sea—to visit foreign countries! To be free—and on your own!"

Henry laughed. "You make it sound like life without a single care. Believe me, it's not all fun and travel!"

They walked down the street arm in arm. After his brother had said goodbye, Edgar returned home feeling sadder and lonelier than ever. Now, as always when he was in deep discouragement, he preferred to sit alone in his room. Thoughts of Elmira came to his mind and helped cheer him up. Seated at his desk, a sheet of paper before him, he tried to find words to picture his affection for her. Soon he began to create a poem dedicated to Elmira, the lines appearing slowly in his heavy, uneven writing.

That evening, as the family sat at dinner, Edgar felt his father's appraising glance. He sensed that Mr. Allan had something on his mind. Toward the end of the meal, his father cleared his throat and looked in Edgar's direction.

"There's something we must talk about," he said, abruptly. "It's a matter of your education."

"Yes, Father," Edgar said. His Aunt Nancy smiled at him while his mother leaned forward to press his hand.

Mr. Allan's fingers drummed on the table. "It's time to think of your future," he said. His face was cold and expressionless as he gazed at Edgar. "I believe you have gone as far as you can in Mr. Burke's school. You must continue your schooling elsewhere."

He hesitated. "I plan to have you enter the University of Virginia. How would you like that?"

Edgar was surprised and thrilled. "The University of Virginia!" he exclaimed. "How wonderful!"

"You should appreciate what your father is doing for you," said Aunt Nancy. "It's not every boy who has a chance to go to the university."

"Oh, I *do* appreciate it," said Edgar, as he thanked his father.

"Then try to act like it," Mr. Allan snapped. "Most of the time you behave like a spoiled child. Come and go when you please—never home when you should be—throw your money away foolishly." He glared at his wife. "I suppose you get those ideas from your mother."

"Oh, John," said Mrs. Allan, pleadingly. "Let's not quarrel any more. This is no time for it. We're discussing Eddie's future."

Barely controlling his anger, John Allan spoke gruffly. "He's not ready for the university yet. He needs tutoring. I'm going to arrange for private tutoring. He shall be withdrawn from Burke's school at once."

Edgar was both pleased and bewildered at the prospect of all these changes. The past year had been an unhappy one in the Allan household. His father seemed always to be in a bad mood, and much of his anger and bitterness was directed at Edgar. By living away from home he could avoid Mr. Allan's continual orders and accusations. But there was something else to be considered. Edgar looked at his mother and touched her hand. He loved her very much. It was difficult to even think of leaving her. She appeared more frail every day, without strength, as though she were gripped by a wasting sickness. What if something happened to her?

"Edgar belongs at the university," said Aunt Nancy, positively. "Perhaps he should prepare to be a lawyer."

"Perhaps," said John Allan, rubbing a hand over his forehead. He pondered while he studied Edgar. "Law could be a good field for him. He has some ability in that direction. We'll see."

"Does he have to travel so far away?" asked Mrs. Allan, her eyes suddenly moist.

"Of course he does," her husband said, impatiently. "How else do you think he can prepare for a profession? He's going on seventeen. He can't stay at home forever."

She sighed deeply and glanced at Edgar. Her relationship with her husband was very strained—far worse than Edgar suspected. It had been that way for some time. Knowing her husband's attitude quite well, she had a strong suspicion of what his future action would be—in a matter that affected Edgar vitally. Mr. Allan had made it plain to her that he did not consider Edgar to be his son. The orphaned boy who had lived in his home all these years and had learned to call him father had never been officially adopted. Mrs. Allan had good reason to fear that her wealthy husband planned to leave nothing to Edgar in his will. All her attempts to persuade him to take a kinder attitude toward Edgar were wasted; in fact, the strong love she and Aunt Nancy had for the boy, and the words she spoke in his favor, only made John Allan more jealous and resentful.

Excited at the turn of events, Edgar's first thought was to share the news with Elmira. As he hurried to her home, he felt dazzled by the possibilities of the future. "Just think," he told Myra, "I am to go to the University of Virginia! I can hardly believe it." In his happiness, the whole story had tumbled out pell-mell.

"It's wonderful for you," said Myra. She smiled as she listened, but soon her face saddened and she clutched his hand. "You'll be leaving Richmond soon," she said. "Oh, Edgar, what will I do then?"

His eyes met hers, and a realization of how deeply he cared for her surged through him. "It'll be some time before I leave," he said. "We'll see each other often."

They walked hand in hand until they came to the garden with the tall linden trees that was Edgar's favorite spot. Here they sat in seclusion and talked of the future.

"Oh, Myra, you must promise to wait for me," said Edgar. "I'll come back. I'll never forget you."

"I will," said Myra. "I'll wait for you forever. I'll never care for anyone but you."

She slipped into his arms and they kissed. To a lonely, sensitive boy like Edgar, she meant everything in the world. She was his first real love. To him the vows they made were deep and eternal —vows that they were pledged to keep until he returned to marry her.

Later they returned to her home where they sat together in the parlor. Myra played the piano while Edgar listened for a while and then sang. He spied a large pad of paper and a pencil on the table and picked them up.

"Draw my picture," said Myra. "Here—I'll pose for you." As she sat there, with her shiny black hair and glowing eyes, his love for her became a sharp pang that seemed to pierce him. He had the ability to capture people's likenesses quickly on paper. Now he sketched and studied her, seeing all the small things about her— the turn of her nose, her round chin, her long eyelashes.

"There," he said, holding up the paper. "All finished."

She looked at it and flushed with pleasure. "It's wonderful, Edgar," she said. "I don't know how you do it so quickly. It looks just like me."

"A present for you," he said with a bow and a laugh.

"The nicest one I've ever received," she answered.

In the days that followed, it seemed to Edgar that time was racing by. Anxious to enter the university well prepared, he worked hard with his tutors. His spare time was spent with Elmira. Although Edgar was only sixteen and Elmira fifteen, they had reached an understanding which they both took seriously. Upon the completion of his studies, Myra was to be his wife. Her family treated Edgar cordially and appeared to have no objection to the match.

Meanwhile, Edgar could not help but be aware that his mother could not bear the thought of his leaving her. The year 1825 drew to an end, and each day brought his departure nearer. To Edgar, it appeared that the prospect of his leaving brought little change in his father's attitude. He was as impatient and as critical as ever. Although John Allan was extremely wealthy, in the past few years he had been inclined to be very grudging of the money he gave Edgar, or of any unusual expenses where Edgar was involved. He had taken to lecturing Edgar about the value of money and to scolding him regularly for spending too freely.

The plans were for Edgar to leave during the first week in February, 1826. Most of his joy and anticipation at going had now vanished. He was gloomy at the thought of leaving Elmira. The dejection and sorrow shown by his mother and his Aunt Nancy had also affected him.

When the day came for his farewells to Elmira, they sat together for the last time in their garden. "I'll write to you often," she told him.

He held her close to him. "I'll love you always," he said. His hand touched her smooth cheek. "Dearest Myra," he said. "Promise me that you'll wait for my return."

"I will," she said softly. "Oh, I will!"

At home Edgar did what he could to cheer up his mother. As he gazed at her, he wondered at how thin and pale her face had grown. Her eyes had dark hollows beneath them. He put his arm around her shoulders. "Are you ill, Mother?" he asked, anxiously. "You don't look well."

She pressed his hand. "Don't worry about me. You know I've never been very strong. It's just that I don't know what the place will be like without you."

"I'll be back for visits," said Edgar. "Charlottesville is not so far away."

"Of course you will." She smiled and tried to give her voice a touch of gayety. "Just think—I'll be driving with you all the way to the university."

On January 19th of that year, Edgar had become seventeen. Sports and outdoor exercise had developed him physically; in this respect he resembled many boys of his own age. But in his periods of seriousness and withdrawal, and above all, in his astonishing imagination and interest in writing, he was not like the others. His individuality and special creative talent had already become evident enough to set him apart from his friends in Richmond.

On the day of departure for Charlottesville, Edgar climbed into the carriage with his mother. His father's goodbyes had been brief and restrained. In shaking Mr. Allan's hand and gazing into his stern face, Edgar thought he glimpsed a little softening and regret at his leaving. He hoped that this was so, and that the man he had learned to call Father would miss him and welcome him home when the time came.

Seated at the front of the carriage, James Hill, the Negro coachman, held the reins in readiness for the signal to start. Edgar leaned out to call to him. "Jim!"

The coachman looked back and smiled. "Yes, Master Edgar."

One hand waved the white envelope toward Jim. It was a last-minute love letter that Edgar had written to Elmira. "Will you—please?" Edgar said.

Jim grinned and nodded. No further words were necessary. He knew that the message was intended for Elmira.

The whip flicked and the carriage started off. Edgar turned to gaze in silence as the Allan home vanished from view. He felt his mother's fingers tighten on his arm and he smiled at her. A disturbing sadness gripped him. Lost in his thoughts, he took no notice of the movements of the carriage. Confused images of the past few days mingled with memories of all his Richmond days and his years in England. Uppermost in his mind was a picture of Elmira as he had last seen her. He could recall the gleam of her eyes when she accepted his going-away present—a mother-of-pearl purse engraved with her initials.

Was it the cold breeze that touched his face or a sudden presentiment that gave him a momentary chill? For a few seconds the future seemed ominous and menacing. Although Edgar could not know it, he and his beloved Myra had lived in a dream world of youth—in a tender, misty world reserved only for the young. Now the joyous fantasies were gone forever—dispelled by the hard realities of adult life.

Already strong forces were working against Elmira and him. Though her parents had known his family for years, and at first had been quite pleased at the prospect of a marriage, John Allan's recent attitude had made them see things in a different light. Edgar was not to be the heir of Allan's fortune. He would not, as they had assumed, become a wealthy young gentleman who could take care of their daughter in the proper fashion. From Allan they may have heard other things—that Edgar was erratic and unreliable. The Roysters had already determined that Edgar was not suited for Elmira. His departure for school was the opportunity they had waited for. This was the time to break up the whole affair—to find another young man for Elmira.

En route to the University of Virginia, Edgar passed the time chatting with his mother, bringing back rich memories of the past and picturing the exciting future. At times, as the carriage lurched along, Elmira's face floated before him. His lips formed the opening of the poem he had written for her, a poem that was permeated with the sadness and the fatality that he could never overcome:

> Thou wast that all to me, love,
>   For which my soul did pine—
> A green isle in the sea, love,
>   A fountain and a shrine,
> All wreathed with fairy fruits and flowers;
>   And all the flowers were mine.

4 · *University Days*

THE university which Edgar entered on February 14, 1826, had been established by Thomas Jefferson. American colleges of the day were mainly under the control of religious sects. To carry out his idea of democratic education, Jefferson planned a new type of university, one without religious affiliation—a school designed for young Americans of all beliefs. At the time Edgar was enrolled, the University of Virginia was less than a year old; its first students had started their classes on March 7, 1825.

Registered in the Schools of Ancient and Modern Languages, Edgar began his studies and his attendance at the lectures given by Professors George Blaettermann and George Long. Edgar's interest had always been in foreign languages; he was to show strong ability in Latin, French, and Italian. University life of the period was quite different from that of today. The classes, starting at seven in the morning, lasted for approximately two hours, and were held six days a week. For the remainder of each day the students were on their own—to study assignments, to read, or to take part in social activities.

Edgar's small, dark room, which he occupied alone, was Number 13 West Range, located on the ground floor. He had always made friends easily and the university was no exception. Unfortunately, Edgar was to find himself in a false situation. He was among young Southern gentlemen, sons of wealthy families, whose parents granted them special allowances and willingly sent them extra amounts to indulge their spending whims. Edgar was also believed to be a member of a wealthy family; his friends assumed that he was heir to John Allan's fortune.

He was unable to tell them the truth—that his father had sent him to school with only $110, although the expenses at the university were estimated to be more than $350 a year. Edgar was forced to pay the entire $110 in advance—$50 for board and $60 for enrollment in two classes. Since he had to pay $15 for room rent, $12 for a bed, and $12 for room furniture, he found himself heavily in debt at the very beginning of his college career. His appeals to John Allan brought him no money; instead, his father answered with scolding, abusing letters. When Edgar watched the other students, noticing how freely they spent their money, he was filled with bitterness and humiliation.

Deep within him was another source of anguish. Alone in his room he dreamed often of his beloved Elmira. But his letters to her had been unanswered. Edgar did not know that Elmira had seen none of his letters. Her father, soon after Edgar had left, had decided that he would choose a well-to-do man to marry his daughter. He had kept all of Edgar's letters from Elmira, and she, not knowing what to believe, thought that Edgar had forgotten her.

In the days that passed, Edgar found himself in what seemed to be a new world. His social life at Richmond had not prepared him for the careless, undisciplined behavior of the young gentlemen at the university. Thomas Jefferson, in his newly opened university, had placed great importance upon student democracy. He believed that the students should govern themselves. The faculty was not expected to assume control over the students' behavior.

Upon arriving at school, Edgar watched the students' antics in amazement. Many of the wealthy young Southerners had already learned to play cards in their home circles. The favorite games, seven-up and loo, were not played for simple amusement; everyone gambled, and unlucky students lost large sums of money. Along with this dissipation went the habit of drinking. Peach-and-honey, a strong alcoholic drink, was popular with the students; drunkenness among the young men was quite common.

Edgar was also astonished upon first viewing the students' behavior. Tempers flared easily, quarrels were frequent, and fights between students were part of normal school life. The Southern gentleman's code of honor, strongly defended, could lead to serious violence. In writing to his father, Edgar described how the campus was in a furor over a feud that had been going on between a student named Turner Dixon and one named Blow. The two had made insulting remarks about each other and had finally taken to writing insults on the university pillars. Edgar and the others were present when the bad feelings reached a climax. A fight broke out between Dixon and Arthur Smith, one of Blow's friends. In the scuffling Dixon picked up a large stone and struck Smith on the head. The enraged Smith then drew a pistol out of his pocket, pointed it at Dixon, and pulled the trigger. Fortunately, the gun missed fire.

The duel, accepted as the gentleman's response to an insult, became common practice at the university. When matters got out of hand, the faculty was forced to step in. In another letter to his father, Edgar told of the vicious fighting he had seen:

We have had a great many fights up here lately— The faculty expelled Wickliffe last night for general bad conduct—but more especially for biting one of the student's arms with whom he was fighting— I saw the whole affair—it took place before my door— Wickliffe was much the stronger but not content with that—after getting the other completely in his power, he began to bite— I saw the arm afterward— and it was really a serious matter— It was bitten from the shoulder to the elbow—and it is likely that pieces of flesh as large as my hand will be obliged to be cut out— He is from Kentucky—the same one that was in suspension when you were up here some time ago— Give my love to Ma and Miss Nancy— I remain, Yours affectionately.

The wild behavior of the students at the university was aggravated by what went on in Charlottesville. In this small town, adjacent to the university, the hotel and boarding-house keepers encouraged the students to spend freely on credit and to run up large bills, for they felt certain that the wealthy parents of the young men would feel obligated to pay such bills. These hotel keepers belonged to the best Southern families; their duties and responsibilities were to provide food for the dormitories and to give the young students, far from home, sound advice and guidance. Instead, they offered the students an unlimited supply of liquor and helped them organize card games.

Surrounded by this type of atmosphere, Edgar was bound to be affected. The friends he had made—all young men provided with large allowances—expected him to join in their activities. Upon arrival at the school he had fallen into debt, and there was no way to avoid getting in deeper and deeper. He had to pay for a servant and to sign bills for food, fuel, and laundry. John Allan refused to send money for these normal expenses. On one occasion, when Edgar sent him an itemized bill for $39, his father mailed a check for $40, telling him to use the extra $1 for spending money! Edgar had no choice but to borrow from moneylenders.

It is true that on one occasion, because of Edgar's participation in military drills, his father sent him a uniform coat, six yards of striped cloth for the trousers, and four pairs of socks. But instead of seeing that his son received desperately needed money for books, Allan sent Edgar a package of three books—the novel *Gil Blas* and a two-volume edition of the *Cambridge Mathematics*. These were of no use at all in the courses Edgar was taking.

Edgar now began to believe that his situation was hopeless. His creditors were demanding money, but he had no way of paying off even the smallest debts. He felt humiliated in the eyes of his friends because he had no spending money. As a result, he turned to gambling, mainly in the hope of winning some money. Aware of the fact that he was gambling recklessly, Edgar still felt that his position forced him to continue; there was always the chance that he might have a streak of good luck.

A seventeen-year-old boy, alone and without the steadying influence of a parent who cared for him, would naturally follow the actions of those around him. Edgar had no previous experience with drinking. Like other boys of his age in Southern homes he had sampled wine; now he found his school friends drinking with an assumed casualness, as though it were the manly thing to do. He wanted to be considered a "regular" fellow also, and so tried to imitate them. Although Edgar drank neither heavily nor regularly, some odd, uncontrollable desire seemed to drive him toward his occasional drinking; and liquor had a strange effect upon him.

In recalling Edgar years later, his friend and classmate Thomas G. Tucker commented upon his gambling and drinking:

Seven-up and loo were his favorite games, for everybody played cards in those days, and he played in so impassioned a manner that it amounted almost to an infatuation. Card-playing and drinking alike were carried on under the spell of impulse or uncontrolled excitement. His passion for strong drink was even then of a most marked and peculiar character. He would always seize the tempting glass, generally unmixed with sugar or water—in fact, perfectly straight—and without the least apparent pleasure swallow the contents, never pausing until the last drop had passed his lips. One glass at a time was all that he could take; but this was sufficient to rouse his whole nervous nature into a state of strongest excitement, which found vent in a continuous flow of wild, fascinated talk that irresistibly enchanted every listener with siren-like power.

While Edgar may have followed the example set by his acquaintances in drinking and card playing, he took no part in the brawling and the gambling that went on in Charlottesville with the connivance of the hotel keepers. The gambling parties became so widespread that, in the spring of 1826, Thomas Jefferson decided that drastic action must be taken. He ordered the civil authorities to find the worst offenders, have them indicted and brought before a Grand Jury. The sheriff and his men appeared suddenly at the university. They waited at the doorway of one of the lecture rooms while the morning roll was being taken; the plan was to serve writs on some of the students. But the word had gotten around, and the students scattered in all directions, some of the most guilty ones bolting through the windows! They made their hideout in a hidden area of the nearby Ragged Mountains. A number of those on the sheriff's list did not return for three days.

Edgar told about the exciting events in a letter to his father:

. . . You have heard no doubt of the disturbances in College— Soon after you left here the Grand Jury met and put the Students in a terrible fright—so much so that the lectures were unattended—and those whose names were upon the Sheriff's list—travelled off into the woods & mountains—taking their beds and provisions along with them—there were about 50 on the list—so you may suppose the College was very well thinn'd. . . .

Edgar went on to explain that this was "the first day of the fright." On the second day, a proclamation was issued by the faculty forbidding "any student under pain of a major punishment to leave his dormitory between the hours of 8 & 10 A.M." Quite aware of the fact that the sheriff would arrive at this time, many of the students again vanished into the woods. Edgar commented, with some humor, that "the fear of the Faculty could not counterbalance that of the Grand Jury."

When the students finally did return, they had to face severe action by the faculty. Edgar reported that "Some were reprimanded —some suspended—and one expelled—James Albert Clarke from Manchester (I went to school with him at Burke's) was suspended for two months. Armstead Carter from this neighborhood for the remainder of the session— And Thomas Barclay for ever—"

It seems clear that Edgar's name was not on the sheriff's list and that he was not guilty of the undisciplined behavior shown by others. At the end of the year, on December 20, 1826, the faculty met for the purpose of considering the charges that "certain Hotel Keepers during the last session had been in the habit of playing at games of chance with the students in their Dormitories—" Edgar was called upon to testify. The faculty records summarize his statement in a few words: *"Edgar Poe never heard until now of any Hotel Keeper playing cards or drinking with students."*

Although Edgar had fallen in with some of the student dissipations, he was still basically a scholar—one who loved learning for its own sake. Literature fascinated him; the creative ideas of all times, from the ancient Greeks down to the romantic poets of his period—these were the writings that stimulated him, giving him a rich background to use in his own creations. At the university library, where Edgar found a good friend in William Wertenbaker, the librarian, he withdrew books in such varied fields as ancient history, Roman and American history, a biography of Washington, a book of French grammar, and a volume by Voltaire. He read much of the history in the original French. His knowledge of the poets of his time, Lord Byron and Thomas Campbell, may have been acquired from privately borrowed or purchased books.

William Wertenbaker never forgot the "handsome young student, perhaps eighteen years of age" who used to come into the library "in search of old French books, principally histories . . ." Recalling Poe's appearance, Wertenbaker described him as "about five feet two or three inches in height, somewhat bandy legged, but in no sense muscular or given to physical exercises." He remembered Poe's "finely marked features, and eyes dark, liquid and expressive." The librarian remarked that Edgar "dressed well and neatly. He was a very attractive companion, genial in his nature . . ." Other descriptions of Edgar indicate that Wertenbaker underestimated Edgar's height.

Miles George, one of Edgar's classmates at the university, remembered him differently. In later years George wrote that Edgar was "of rather a delicate & slender mould. His legs not bowed, or so slightly as to escape notice, and did not detract either from the symmetry of his person or the ease and grace of his carriage— To be practical & unpoetical I think his weight was between 130 & 140 pounds."

Both students and instructors came to have a high regard for Edgar's scholastic ability. His classmates, who needed long hours of study to learn the difficult passages in French or Latin, envied Edgar for his ease and quickness in covering the same material.

When Edgar entered the lecture room, those who knew him well would watch in amused anticipation while he made his "on-the-spot" preparations.

"I'll bet that's the first time he's looked at the pages," a student would whisper to another. They would watch while Edgar leafed through the book at high speed.

On most occasions the students were right. With his keen, active brain and remarkable memory, Edgar could scan the assignment a few moments before class and grasp all the important details. When Professors Blaettermann or Long would call out "Mr. Poe!", Edgar would stand up eagerly. He loved to recite in public, to appear before a group of listeners. Attention, and the eyes of others upon him, acted as a stimulus, arousing him and exciting all his creative energy. Although his preparations were usually brief, his recitations were excellent and often earned the professors' praise. Languages had always interested and challenged him; for Blaettermann, a man not easily impressed, Edgar even demonstrated a surprising ability in Italian. His translation of a difficult passage from the works of *Tasso* drew a commendation from the professor.

On December 15, 1826, when the results of the examinations in the School of Ancient Languages were posted, Edgar's name was high on the list of students who excelled in Latin. In the examination list of the Senior French Class, Edgar was included within the small group of eight students who were commended as "excellent."

Through closer acquaintance, his friends had become well aware of the special fascination Edgar could exert on an audience. In his small room, Number 13 West Range, he would read or tell stories to a group of listeners. Here he was experimenting—trying out the early forms of poems that would later appear in print, or shaping the characters and the plots of his weird, morbid stories. To the ready listeners Edgar may have sounded the words, which he was still polishing and revising, of his poem *Tamerlane*. The narrative of the lowly shepherd, driven by fierce desire, who rose to occupy a Mongol throne and then to realize in final bitterness that his overpowering ambition had destroyed love, was certain to thrill the friends who gathered about the young poet. The flames that leaped high in the fireplace to throw odd shadows on the walls of his room gave Edgar the atmosphere he needed when it came time to weave his strange tales. His young audience must have imagined the touch of icy fingers and trembled with sudden chills as he spun grotesque stories of terror and death.

But Edgar was not one to spend all his spare time indoors. Often he felt the need of the outdoors and the urgency to be alone, to meditate and to brood. Then he would leave his confining room and walk briskly away from the university, his eyes upon the dark outlines of the Ragged Mountains. Once he arrived in the mountains' shelter, he would seek to lose himself in a world of beauty and peace. Never to be forgotten, his retreat provided the background for *A Tale of the Ragged Mountains*. To Edgar the scenery was pictured as having "a delicious aspect of dreary desolation." The memories of his ramblings "among the chain of wild and dreary hills" and of the discovery of secret nooks that made the everyday life of frustration and worry seem far away, became part of Edgar's storehouse of rich images—images that were to color his strange stories of the future.

A Tale of the Ragged Mountains did not appear in print until April, 1844, but its very first lines signaled a return to the painful past and the brief days at college:

"During the fall of the year 1827, while residing near Charlottes-ville, Virginia, I casually made the acquaintance of Mr. Augustus Bedloe."

Here, as in many of his tales, Edgar loved to write in the first person, to live among the feelings of fear, horror, and the supernatural that seemed to sprout with every scratch of his pen. If he could not be the main character, evil, warped, self-driven toward a terrible destruction, he would compromise for the second best. He would be an on-looker in his stories, watching and recording the odd, unearthly events. He observes his *"Mr. Augustus Bedloe"* and his astonishing journey into the Ragged Mountains. In his creation of Bedloe, Edgar showed that he could wander into strange paths—far beyond those taken by other writers of his time. Description and characterization of grotesque creatures, like Bedloe, moving in bizarre worlds—these became his trademark:

Of his family I could obtain no satisfactory account. Whence he came, I never ascertained. Even about his age—although I call him a young gentleman—there was something which perplexed me in no little degree. He certainly *seemed* young—and he made a point of speaking about his youth—yet there were moments when I should have had little trouble in imagining him a hundred years of age. But in no regard was he more peculiar than in his personal appearance. He was singularly tall and thin. He stooped much. His limbs were exceedingly long and emaciated. His forehead was broad and low. His complexion was absolutely bloodless. His mouth was large and flexible, and his teeth were more widely uneven, although sound, than I had ever before seen teeth in a human head. The expression of his smile, however, was by no means unpleasing, as might be supposed; but it had no variation whatever. It was one of profound melancholy—of a phaseless and unceasing gloom.

49

Here Edgar displayed his ability for observing the smallest details and his genius of focusing upon only those details that would combine to produce the effects of strangeness and terror that he wanted. One of his favorites was the human eye; he understood that the writer who hopes to create a weird impression must concentrate upon the odd shapes and motions of the eye. Bedloe's eyes were "abnormally large, and round like those of a cat." Edgar used a master's touch to picture them:

The pupils, too, upon any accessation or diminution of light, underwent contraction or dilation, just such as is observed in the feline tribe. In moments of excitement the orbs grew bright to a degree almost inconceivable; seeming to emit luminous rays, not of a reflected but of an intrinsic lustre, as does a candle or the sun; yet their ordinary condition was so totally vapid, filmy, and dull, as to convey the idea of the eyes of a long-interred corpse.

The wealthy Augustus Bedloe, an invalid as the result of "a long series of neuralgic attacks," has placed himself under the care of Dr. Templeton, a practicer of Mesmerism. The doctor succeeds in putting his patient into hypnotic "sleeps" and developing "a very distinct and strongly marked *rapport,* or magnetic relation" between them. Later, this relationship leads to an incident of strange communication—out of time and place.

The eccentric Bedloe, already "sensitive, excitable, enthusiastic," had turned to "the habitual use of morphine, which he swallowed in great quantity. . . . It was his practice to take a very large dose of it immediately after breakfast each morning—" Bedloe would then set off for his daily trip into the Ragged Mountains. In describing how Bedloe entered a gorge and followed the winding pass, Edgar drew from his memories of many rambles to the secret places of the mountains:

The solitude seemed absolutely virgin. I could not help believing that the green sods and the gray rocks upon which I trod had been trodden never before by the foot of a human being. So entirely secluded, and in fact inaccessible, except through a series of accidents, is the entrance of the ravine, that it is by no means impossible that I was indeed the first adventurer—the very first and sole adventurer who had ever penetrated its recesses.

Soon Bedloe finds himself transported back in time to an unfamiliar far-Eastern city where fierce, violent action is occurring. As the story ends, the reader may accept Bedloe as a bizarre creature of reincarnation or consider the entire incident as nothing more than a hallucination—caused by hypnotism and drugs.

Such was the wildly imaginative tale set against the peaceful seclusion of a well-remembered spot—the Ragged Mountains. Other university scenes and experiences would appear in future stories. But with the passing of the days Edgar found his situation unbearable. Completely without funds, and subjected to abuse in letters from John Allan, Edgar turned more to gambling and drinking. In desperation he wrote to his childhood friend, James Galt, who had inherited a sizable sum under the will of his uncle, William Galt. Edgar's request for money was refused.

Edgar's gambling debts and the amount he owed to the merchants at Charlottesville, plus his unpaid bill for a servant at the university, now came to a frightening total. In the fall of 1826, these accounts became due—and somehow John Allan learned that Edgar's debts were even heavier than had been suspected. Enraged, he made a hurried trip to the university. There the exasperated Scotsman discovered the true situation: his son owed more than $2,000 in gambling debts alone!

"Those I have no intention of paying," he told Edgar. To Allan, his son's conduct was unforgivable.

Edgar's explanations went unheard and his protests only increased his father's anger. "Your days at the university are over." John Allan, in a fury, hurled the words as though a sentence were being pronounced. "I'm bringing you home at the end of the term!"

The fact that his son had made honors lists in Latin and French and was considered by the professors to be an outstanding student made no difference to Allan. Nor was he capable of admitting that his own stinginess and lack of understanding were the real causes of his son's difficulties.

Edgar, who had already suffered continual embarrassment in the days that had passed, was now to be further humiliated before his friends; he was to withdraw in disgrace, owing unpaid debts. In addition, under the laws of Virginia, these debts were legally due. Warrants would soon be issued for their collection, and Edgar could face imprisonment.

Toward the end of December, 1826, when the other students were preparing to return home for the holidays to warm family circles and gay celebrations, Edgar walked gloomily back to his room to prepare for his farewell to the university. With him was his friend, William Wertenbaker, the librarian.

As they entered the cold, dark room, Edgar felt a shiver run through him. "The fire is almost out," he said. He glanced about, once more feeling the despair that had been like a permanent companion to him. Firewood was expensive and he had neither money nor credit. His mood of indifference and lethargy flamed into rebellion. His eye fixed upon a small table. Why not, he thought. The furniture was his; he would never have use for it again. He seized the table and began pounding it against the floor. It splintered and the legs buckled. Edgar broke them off. "Now we'll have some fire," he said, while Wertenbaker watched him curiously. He piled the fragments into the fireplace.

Edgar lit the tallow candles that he kept in the room, started the flames going again, and within minutes had a warm blaze lighting up the room. The two sat silent for a while, staring at the red and yellow shapes that flared in the fireplace. In Edgar's mind the regrets over his conduct at school—the thoughts of what he had done and what he might have done—appeared in the form of ghastly images.

"I've thrown away a lot of money," he said in a low voice. It was as though he spoke to himself, hardly conscious of the librarian's presence.

"Not any more than the others did," Wertenbaker said, consolingly.

"Over two thousand dollars," said Edgar.

"They're mainly gaming debts, aren't they?" his friend asked.

"Gaming debts or not," Edgar said emphatically, "I feel honor bound to pay them. I intend to pay every cent of them."

After they had talked for more than an hour, Wertenbaker arose to go. The two stood facing each other, awkward in the grip of sudden emotion.

Wertenbaker held out his hand and Edgar clasped it. "I'll see you tomorrow before the coach leaves," said Edgar. He spoke in a low, despondent voice.

"Of course," said Wertenbaker, smiling. "Cheer up; I'm sure everything will turn out well."

Edgar smiled bravely in return. When the door had closed behind his friend, he sat down again before the fire. Even a pretense of optimism was impossible. He was flooded with the deepest gloom. He felt that he had wasted his past opportunities; in his guilt at his college dissipations was he imagining himself as the evil *William Wilson* who appeared in later years in his story? In the first-person writing that he used so often, Edgar wrote about his "family character": "I grew self-willed, addicted to the wildest caprices, and a prey to the most ungovernable passions."

Although the main settings are Eton and Oxford, it seems clear that Edgar was recalling all the wildness, drinking, and gambling that had surrounded him at the University of Virginia. William Wilson's behavior was created from observation and experience, but he acquires exaggerated vices. Edgar writes, "I invited a small party of the most dissolute students to a secret carousal in my chambers." The group met at a late hour, for the debaucheries "were to be faithfully protracted until morning." Edgar hints at "more dangerous seductions" and describes Wilson as "madly flushed with cards and intoxication."

As the setting shifts to Oxford, the evil Wilson tells how he falls lower and lower:

. . . I spurned even the common restraints of decency in the mad infatuation of my revels. . . .

. . . I had, even here, so utterly fallen from the gentlemanly estate, as to seek acquaintance with the vilest arts of the gambler by profession, and having become an adept in his despicable science, to practice it habitually as a means of increasing my already enormous income at the expense of the weak-minded among my fellow-collegians.

Thus at Oxford, "the most dissolute university in Europe," Edgar establishes the wealthy Wilson and supplies him with unlimited funds for every vice. In his vivid imagination he has gone far beyond any dissipations he ever contemplated at the University of Virginia. But in creating the spendthrift Wilson, was Edgar building a dream—to compensate for his own penniless days at school?

But now the real university days were over. What were the thoughts that ran through his mind as he sat alone in his last evening on campus? Certainly he must have wondered about Elmira and why she had failed to answer his letters. How would she act toward him when he returned? Had she forgotten him already?

While he brooded, he set about packing his belongings and disposing of unneeded items. Numerous papers, including rough drafts of his own poems, were hurled into the flames. With the manuscripts packed in his trunk may have been two of his long poems, *Tamerlane* and *Al Aaraaf*. These and some shorter poems were soon to appear in print.

Edgar had no illusions about what he would face at home. Only eight months of college education had been granted to him; he would never again take part in university life. John Allan had already made his wishes plain: his son was to go to work in his counting-room or warehouse. But Edgar had also made up his mind, and a clash of wills was certain. He would leave the Allan house at the first opportunity.

The Christmas holiday season, a time for families to be united again in love and understanding, brought Edgar home to Richmond. To other students the prospect of exchanging a small, cold room at the university for the warmth and comfort of the family circle was something to be anticipated. But in December, 1826, as Edgar walked up the steps of the Allan home, he was in the grip of conflicting emotions. He was eager to see his mother and his Aunt Nancy—and fearful of what might take place when he met his father.

At the open door he found his mother waiting. "Oh, Edgar," she cried. "Welcome home!"

She kissed him, and he put an arm around her shoulder. Then he stood off and looked at her. "It's nice to be home again," he said, smiling.

"You've grown taller and thinner," she said.

Edgar's first joy turned to concern as he studied his mother's haggard face. He moved forward to touch her cheek with his fingers. "Have you been ill, Mother?" he asked.

"I've been the same." She attempted a smile. "Don't worry about me. You're home for the holidays." She drew him close to her. "Oh, Edgar—I hope so much that things will go well."

He knew she was thinking of his father and that she shared his worries. "How is Father?" he asked. "And how is Aunt Nancy?"

"They're both fine," she said. "Your father will be home later." She looked at him anxiously for a moment and then her eyes lit up with gayety. "We're having a Christmas Eve party to celebrate your return."

Throughout the long ride from Charlottesville, memories of Elmira had taken control of Edgar's mind, and her face had seemed like a warm, smiling picture before him, her lips urging him to hurry home. Now he suddenly felt that he couldn't wait any longer.

"If you don't mind, Mother—" he said, hesitantly, "there's someone I must visit."

She studied his face, her eyes soft with understanding. "Why don't you wait until tomorrow?" she asked. "Your father will want to talk to you when he comes home."

"I'll be back soon," Edgar said.

As he turned and walked toward the door, his mother called out, "Edgar—there's something—"

He looked around. "Yes, Mother?"

"Well—" She sighed and shook her head. "It's nothing. I'll be waiting for you when you return."

On his way to Elmira's house, Edgar found that each step that brought him nearer to the girl he loved increased his anxiety. At school he had been puzzled and worried over Elmira's failure to answer his letters. Now it seemed to him that his mother had looked at him strangely. There was something wrong; his heart sank as the thought came to him. Could it be that the girl who had promised to marry him had changed her mind? Or that she cared more for somebody else?

At the Royster home he found more to mystify him. Elmira was not there. The answers were vague and evasive. Nobody knew when she would return. Edgar was not asked to come in and wait. The place where he had been warmly welcomed before, where Elmira had played the piano, they both had sung, and he had tried tunes on the flute, now appeared to be the home of strangers. He left, his mind in a daze, feeling that somehow, in the few short months he had been away from Richmond, the entire world had changed.

Mrs. Allan had known that he would return in grief and dismay. "I don't understand," he said. "I don't understand . . ." She told him what she had learned. He must not take his romance with Elmira too seriously. In fact, it would be best to forget her. Her parents were arranging for Elmira to marry an older man— a Mr. Shelton who was already successfully established and could provide for Elmira.

To Edgar's worries about how his father would receive him was now added a disappointment almost too heavy to bear. His dream about a future with Elmira had supported him during the uncertainty of his university days; it had become the one thing in his life that he could count on. Now that dream was vanishing, and for Edgar all that the homecoming meant was the scenes he dreaded—the bickering with Mr. Allan and the angry complaints about money spent and gambled away.

Christmas Eve, and its party celebrating Edgar's return from school, could not change his mood of deepest gloom. The arrival of Tom Bolling, one of Edgar's school friends, whose family owned a plantation near Richmond, cheered him up somewhat. Later the house was filled with friends whom Edgar had known from childhood, who came to welcome him home and exchange holiday greetings.

In their first meeting, Mr. Allan had been coldly polite and restrained. As they shook hands, Edgar tried to be cordial toward the stern-faced man who faced him. The memories of how kind Allan had been to him in the early years came back. Edgar wondered why all the warmth between father and son had disappeared. He could not understand the man's stinginess—his refusal to give Edgar the allowance that other university students were receiving from their parents.

For some time John Allan had been troubled with a lame foot. In walking about he found it necessary to use a cane.

"I hope you're feeling better," Edgar said. "Your leg—" he added, awkwardly. "Does it bother you much?"

"I'm getting along." Mr. Allan sounded the few words in his dry, expressionless way. A light of annoyance touched his eyes and he seemed on the verge of saying something else, but changed his mind. He turned about abruptly and stamped away, his cane tapping on the floor.

Edgar stared after him, understanding what the gesture meant. His father had many things to say; there would be bitter comments and accusations about his son's behavior. They were certain to come later. But now the two were in the midst of a holiday truce.

The New Year, 1827, arrived, and Edgar wandered about the house, fretful and discouraged. On January 19th, he would be eighteen. He had a right to expect that some plans should be made for his future. But his father chose to ignore the entire matter. They quarreled frequently, with Mr. Allan making insulting comments about his son's laziness and idleness. Yet, he also made it plain that there was no hope of Edgar's returning to the university.

As the wasted days passed, and Edgar realized that his father was not at all concerned about a career or a profession for his son, he tried to make some of his own plans. He remembered that at one time he had been interested in being a lawyer. "I'd like to prepare myself in law," he told his mother. But his father gave no encouragement, refusing even to discuss the topic.

Soon other matters arose to add to Edgar's problems. Mr. Allan had insisted, on numerous occasions, that he had no intention of paying any of Edgar's debts—even those that his son had been forced to incur because of normal university expenses. Threatening letters from creditors and warrants began arriving at the house. Edgar now faced the prospect of being put in jail for non-payment of his debts. Whenever he appealed to his father, the answer was always the same: Allan made bitter remarks about Edgar's extravagant spending and his wild gambling. He could not or would not see that part of the blame lay with him. His miserliness and refusal to give his son a reasonable allowance had given Edgar no choice but to borrow from everybody and to live on credit.

The month of February brought no change in Edgar's relationship with his father. Edgar now found the situation unbearable. The quarrels went on, with Mr. Allan exploding in a furious climax: his son was ungrateful, he had disgraced him with his drinking and gambling, and, as far as Allan was concerned, he could get out of the house. Edgar had already made up his mind that he could not continue living in a home where he received constant accusations and insults, so, on March 19th, he said goodbye to his mother and set off aimlessly through the town of Richmond. He had little money and felt deeply shamed at the thought of turning to his boyhood friends, explaining the sorry details of his home life and asking their parents to take him in. The only retreat left to him was a public place—the Court House Tavern in Richmond.

There he sat in anguish through the long hours and finally decided to write a letter to his father. In the letter, after explaining that he had no choice but to leave, Edgar poured out the agony of the past months of frustration.

. . . My determination is at length taken—to leave your house and endeavor to find some place in the wide world, where I will be treated—not as *you* have treated me. . . .

. . . I have heard you say (when you little thought I was listening and therefore must have said it in earnest) that you had no affection for me— You have moreover ordered me to quit your house, and are continually upbraiding me with eating the bread of idleness, when you yourself were the only person to remedy the evil by placing me to some business— You take delight in exposing me before those whom you think likely to advance my interest in this world . . .

The next day Edgar reached a decision which circumstances forced him to take—he must leave Richmond as soon as possible. There was no employment for him in town and nobody to turn to for assistance. Unable to wait for an answer to his first letter, he wrote a second, more desperate, letter to his father. He implored Mr. Allan to send the trunk containing his clothes and books, and above all, to send money for a passage to Boston and a little extra to support him for a month. By then, Edgar explained, "I shall be enabled to place myself in some situation where I may not only obtain a livelihood, but lay by a sum which one day or another will support me at the University. . . ."

Edgar wrote that he was in the "greatest necessity, not having tasted food since yesterday morning. I have nowhere to sleep at night, but roam about the streets . . ." Toward the close of the letter Edgar requested, "Give my love to all at home," and closed with the piteous postscript, "I have not one cent in the world to provide any food."

The cost of passage to Boston was only twelve dollars; yet Edgar waited in vain for Mr. Allan to send him any money. He had explained that he intended to leave on Saturday, March 24th. As he wandered through the streets of Richmond, wretched and hungry, he carried with him the constant fear of sudden arrest, for he felt certain that the numerous warrants issued against him for unpaid debts would lead to his imprisonment. Some time ago Edgar had decided that it was safest for him to take an alias. His foreign language studies at the university and his love of French led him naturally to think of a French name: his choice was "Henri Le Rennét."

The scheduled Saturday sailing for Boston drew near. Edgar had reached the last stages of hope when a secret message was delivered to him. It was from his mother. She enclosed the money he needed and sent him her deepest love. The unhappy "Henri Le Rennét" boarded the ship for Boston—the city of his birth. It was to be the city in which his literary career was launched.

5 · *Independence*, Tamerlane, *and Deepening Sorrow*

In April, 1827, a young man stood gazing into the window of a small printing shop at 70 Washington Street in Boston. Passersby who scrutinized the eighteen-year-old Poe with any interest would have observed a youth of medium height and build, about five feet, eight inches tall, with searching gray eyes, brown hair somewhat uncombed, and a fair complexion. In spite of the uncertainty of the future, the fact that he was on his own in a huge city with little money and no prospect of employment, Edgar found the sights and sounds of Boston thrilling. He had wandered through the city for hours, rubbing elbows with people in the crowded streets and staring in fascination at the displays in the windows of the quaint stores.

The sign CALVIN F. S. THOMAS . . . PRINTER had drawn him like a magnet. Peering into the store window, he could see the cases and catch the metallic gleam of type faces. In the back of the small shop he could glimpse the outlines of the printing presses.

As Edgar's glance turned away, he became aware of a young man standing in the doorway of the shop and smiling at him. "Do you have some printing work to be done?" the young man asked.

Edgar returned his smile and then shook his head hesitantly. "No," he said. "At least, not at this time."

"I do all kinds of work," the young man said eagerly. He seemed about Edgar's age. "If it's book or job printing you want —I do them both. Pamphlets, catalogues, cards . . . My prices are quite reasonable."

Edgar shook his head again. "I'd like to have something printed, but I couldn't . . . not now." He gazed in through the open door of the small shop.

"Would you like to see the place?" the young man asked. "Why don't you come in?" In his eagerness he almost swept Edgar into the store.

Edgar looked around, noticing the neatly arranged fonts of type and the stacks of paper. His eye was caught by the large letters on a placard which reminded him of the shop owner's name: PRINTING . . . CALVIN F. S. THOMAS

He looked at the young man doubtfully. It didn't seem possible that so young a person was the owner of a shop. "Are you . . . Mr. Thomas?" he asked.

The other nodded, his face lighting up. "I've just bought the shop," he said. He waved an arm excitedly. "Isn't it fine? It has everything that you need for any kind of job printing." He gave Edgar a closer look. "Do you live in town?"

"I've just arrived from Richmond," Edgar said. He considered for a moment. "My name . . . is Henri Le Rennét."

They both laughed and shook hands. "Henri," the young man repeated. "And I hope you'll call me Calvin."

They walked around the shop with Calvin proudly showing Edgar all the equipment and explaining its use. After a while, as they sat chatting, Calvin looked at him curiously. "If you don't mind my asking," he said, "when I first talked about printing I had an impression that you had something in mind—that there was something you wanted to have printed."

"There is," Edgar admitted. "But there's no point in talking about it." He glanced at Calvin and flushed. "To tell you the truth, I have no money to pay for it."

Included in the few belongings he had carried with him was a precious folder containing all of his completed poems. A number of these had been written when he was only thirteen or fourteen years old. His favorite one was a long, imaginative poem about a Mongol emperor whom Edgar had named *Tamerlane*.

"Well," said Calvin regretfully, "perhaps you can have it printed later. I'll be glad to do it at any time. Do you plan to stay in Boston —and look for employment?"

Edgar nodded glumly. He felt certain that he would not easily find employment. He had never thought that there was a chance of having his poems printed. But now the very prospect filled him with a desperate eagerness. To see his own creations on a printed page—to see the title **TAMERLANE** in bold capitals! No thrill could ever equal this! He studied the gleaming metal fonts. So near—and yet so inaccessible. Somehow, no matter what happened, he must find a way to print a book of his poems.

In the days that followed, he was often at Calvin's shop. The search for employment had been unsuccessful. He existed on the remainder of the money his mother had sent him, but even so, the temptation of seeing his work in print was too strong to resist. One day he walked into the shop, his mind made up. Under one arm he carried his folder of poems.

"When can you start the printing of my poems?" he asked. Having already discussed the matter with Calvin several times, he knew that his friend would charge him little more than the cost of the printing.

Calvin stared at Edgar, his face a picture of both pleasure and surprise. He was eager to print the poems, but well aware of the fact that his friend "Henri's" only means of support was his tiny hoard of money. "Are you sure you want to go ahead with it?" he questioned.

"Yes," said Edgar. He held out the folder. "Please begin as soon as you can. And I want to give you some money in advance."

Calvin smiled. "That's all right—if you wish. But it won't be necessary. I'll start the first thing tomorrow morning. We'll count on printing fifty copies."

Edgar's eyes shone with excitement. "I'll be here to help you— the first thing in the morning!"

The next day, Calvin began setting the type for Edgar's first book of poetry, a collection that included *Tamerlane* and a number of smaller poems. It can easily be imagined that Edgar spent much time in the shop, watching his little book take shape. From him came careful instructions on punctuation and on the arrangement of the lines, and when the first proofs were pulled from the press, Edgar must have made many of the corrections.

A first book by a young author could not be complete without a Preface. Edgar's Preface offered explanations and an apology:

The greater part of the poems which compose this little volume were written in the year 1821–22, when the author had not completed his fourteenth year. They were of course not intended for publication; why they are now published concerns no one but himself. Of the smaller pieces very little need be said, they perhaps savour too much of egotism; but they were written by one too young to have any knowledge of the world but from his own breast. . . .

Is there any way to picture the thrill that Edgar must have experienced when the first copy of the thin book was placed in his hands? As satisfying as it was, he had sacrificed part of the pride of creation by a decision that could have been made only with difficulty. The author of *Tamerlane and Other Poems* was to remain anonymous. No name appeared on the front cover or title page.

The cover was certain to attract the reader's eye. Its rectangular engraving was made up of heavy black scroll work. Within the decoration were the lines of print, with TAMERLANE in large capitals at the top. Above the center, where the author's name normally appeared, was the statement:

BY A BOSTONIAN

Beneath this, for his dedication Edgar chose two lines written by the poet William Cowper:

> Young heads are giddy, and young hearts are warm,
> And make mistakes for manhood to reform.

Twice in the same work Edgar had referred to his youth and impulsiveness. His understanding of a young person's tendency to make mistakes, and his apologies for his egotism and lack of knowledge, actually show an unusual maturity for an eighteen-year-old. In his university days he had shown remorse and a painful awareness of his dissipations, even though he felt that circumstances had left him no choice. All through life he was fated to suffer agonies over the knowledge of his own faults and failures, while at the same time rebelling against the terrible punishment that he did not deserve.

Why was *Tamerlane* printed anonymously, with the cryptic phrase "By a Bostonian"? Was the young man with the alias of "Henri Le Rennét" afraid to place a name on his poems because of the warrants that had been issued against him? The reason appears a logical one for his actions. His choice of "a Bostonian" may be explained by his pride in the city of his birth and the fact that, as a literary center, it had more prestige than Richmond.

As *Tamerlane* opens, we find the powerful Mongol emperor, now dying, telling the story of his life to a holy friar. The theme is one of regret over a wasted life with a mad pursuit of power; of conquered empires and of a sovereign's throne. Tamerlane had risen from his birth as a lowly peasant to earn a crown in fierce battle, and finally rule with a savage tyranny:

> A cottager, I marked a throne
> Of half the world as all my own,
> And murmured at such a lowly lot—

The dying man realizes too late that he has forfeited the pure love that he shared as a youth with his childhood sweetheart,

62

which he now values far more than all his grandeur and pride in conquest:

> We grew in age—and love—together—
> Roaming the forest, and the wild;
> My breast her shield in wintry weather—
> And, when the friendly sunshine smiled.
> And she would mark the opening skies,
> I saw no Heaven—but in her eyes,

To Edgar, the romantic theme was as natural as all the dreams of youth; it stemmed from his intense idealism. He explained that he wanted "to expose the folly of even *risking* the best feelings of the heart at the shrine of ambition."

At the end the tortured monarch asks in anguish:

> How was it that Ambition crept,
> Unseen, amid the revels there,
> Till growing bold, he laughed and leapt
> In the tangles of Love's very hair?

Edgar still brooded over his loss of Elmira Royster. Was it possible that, in condemning the ambition which destroys love, he was blaming himself? Did he believe that, by leaving Richmond to enroll at the university, he had deserted Elmira—that, like Tamerlane, he had sacrificed a pure love in his pursuit of ambition? In the poem *Tamerlane,* perhaps Edgar was bitterly regretting the love he had left behind, when he wrote:

> Why did I leave it, and, adrift,
> Trust to the fire within, for light?

The knowledge that he had lost Elmira, and the certainty of her marriage to the wealthy A. Barrett Shelton, may have prompted Edgar to write another poem of despair, the short *Song,* which was printed in his little book. The first two stanzas tell of his sadness:

> I saw thee on thy bridal day—
> When a burning blush came o'er thee,
> Though happiness around thee lay,
> The world all love before thee:
>
> And in thine eye a kindly light
> (Whatever it might be)
> Was all on Earth my aching sight
> Of loveliness could see.

Calvin and Edgar completed the printing of *Tamerlane and Other Poems* early in May, 1827. It was actually a small pamphlet, 6⅜ by 4⅛ inches, containing about forty pages. Between forty and fifty copies of the yellow-covered booklet were printed; it sold for twelve and one-half cents. There was no money to pay for its distribution, and only two copies were sent out to magazine reviewers. How thrilled the unhappy young poet, who starved himself to pay for the small pamphlet, might have been if he could have foreseen the future! Most of the copies of Edgar's first book disappeared. Of the first edition of *Tamerlane and Other Poems,* bearing the heavy black letters **BOSTON: CALVIN F. S. THOMAS . . . . PRINTER . . . . 1827** on the cover, only four priceless copies exist today. In 1919 more than $11,000 was paid for one of these!

The excitement of watching his poems appear in print may have helped Edgar forget his desperate situation. But now, with his money gone and no hope of obtaining more, he was forced to face reality. In his earlier years, he had enjoyed donning a uniform and playing at soldiering. When he had been visited by his brother Henry, who was in the Navy, he had envied Henry's freedom and his opportunities to visit foreign lands; at that time he had half-wished to be in the Navy or the Army. Although Edgar may have realized by now that a regimented life was not for him, he had no other choice. So, on May 26, 1827, he enlisted in the United States Army, falsely stating his name as Edgar A. "Perry," and his age as twenty-two. He was scheduled to remain in Boston for some time, and was assigned to Battery H of the First Artillery in Fort Independence, Boston Harbor.

Edgar listed his occupation as "clerk," and it appears that he did some type of clerical work in the Army. During this period he wrote letters to his mother and corresponded with his brother Henry in Baltimore. The rumor at home was that Edgar may have gone abroad. Edgar himself may have been responsible for this rumor; it is believed that he dated some of his letters from foreign countries, including "St. Petersburg, Russia." To Henry, Edgar wrote regularly, telling him sadly of the broken love affair with Elmira and sending him a copy of *Tamerlane.*

On October 31, 1827, Battery H left Boston Harbor, its new destination Fort Moultrie, on Sullivan's Island in Charleston Harbor, South Carolina. The moving of a complete Battery took some time, and Edgar did not arrive at his new station until November

18th. For the next month he was to experience a new, exciting phase in his life. Old Fort Moultrie was located on Sullivan's Island, a sliver of land that had become a retreat for birds, insects, and the sea-turtles who occupied its sandy soil. Always one who was fascinated by nature and, as in Charlottesville, loved to take long solitary rambles, Edgar roamed the island, observing the colorful animal life and wondering at the strange vegetation. Nothing escaped his curious gaze; he memorized the lines and shades of this tiny island. And he thrilled over the knowledge of the island's rich past. Pirate ships had lain at anchor in the bay, and on the island he could imagine the buccaneers in bloody battles with cutlasses and swords and dream of buried chests of jewels, silver, and gold.

To the boy who remembered and wrote about his days in England, it was inevitable that Sullivan's Island and its treasures should be stored away in all its detail, saved for the day when its pirate-haunted beaches and woodland might supply the setting for an ingenious tale. The moment came, and Edgar drew upon the unlimited storehouse of his memory; what he had seen and loved of nature he could never forget, and fifteen years later he wrote:

Many years ago, I contracted an intimacy with a Mr. William Legrand. He was of an ancient Huguenot family, and had once been wealthy; but a series of misfortunes had reduced him to want. To avoid the mortification consequent upon his disasters, he left New Orleans, the city of his forefathers, and took up his residence at Sullivan's Island, near Charleston, South Carolina.

Here, in his famous story, *The Gold Bug,* Edgar chose to make Sullivan's Island the setting for a fascinating story that combined elements of the strange, the mysterious, and the macabre. Detective work, pirates, hidden treasure, and violent death are Edgar's creations, taking place on an island that reappeared with the details of a photograph:

This island is a very singular one. It consists of little else than the sea sand, and is about three miles long. Its breadth at no point exceeds a quarter of a mile. It is separated from the mainland by a scarcely perceptible creek, oozing its way through a wilderness of reeds and slime, a favorite resort of the marsh-hen. The vegetation, as might be supposed, is scant, or at least dwarfish. No trees of any magnitude are to be seen. Near the western extremity, where Fort Moultrie stands, and where are some miserable frame buildings, tenanted, during summer, by the fugitives from Charleston dust and fever, may be found, indeed, the

65

bristly palmetto; but the whole island, with the exception of this western point, and a line of hard, white beach on the sea-coast, is covered with a dense undergrowth of the sweet myrtle so much prized by the horticulturists of England. The shrub here often attains the height of fifteen or twenty feet, and forms an almost impenetrable coppice, burdening the air with its fragrance.

During his stay at Sullivan's Island, Edgar found that Army life permitted him unlimited time for his explorations. Once the routine exercises were over and he had completed his clerical work, he was free to roam the barren island or to relax on the sandy beaches. His curious mind, as always, was hard at work discovering, examining, and hoarding everything of value—images, impressions, data. But what of his writing? Did anything take shape on paper—revisions of old poems or perhaps some new ones? It would be hard to conceive of Edgar passing any lengthy period without some creative attempt.

Either among his few possessions, or stored in his memory, were lines of an unusually imaginative poem. He had given it the odd title of *Al Aaraaf*, taken, as he later explained, from the Al Aaraaf of the Arabians, "a medium between Heaven and Hell where men suffer no punishment, but yet do not attain that tranquil & even happiness which they suppose to be characteristic of heavenly enjoyment." This mysterious Al Aaraaf was located by Edgar in a star discovered by Tycho Brahe, a sixteenth-century Danish astronomer. Perhaps, in idle hours on the island or in his barracks, Edgar turned to lengthening and polishing the poem. It was soon to appear in print.

In the passing months Edgar had made several attempts to start a correspondence with Mr. Allan. His father had not replied to him directly, although there is evidence that he knew that Edgar was in the Army. In his letters, Edgar had inquired about his mother's health and sent his love to her. Meanwhile, new orders had been issued to Battery H. The outfit was scheduled to depart for Fortress Monroe, Virginia, some time in December, 1828. Edgar's sixteen months as an enlisted man in the Regular Army had brought him to a state of deep discouragement. The prospect of finishing out the remainder of his period of five years was unthinkable. In this unhappy situation, the only person who could aid him was Mr. Allan. Edgar wrote appealing letters to his father, humbling himself and apologizing for his conduct at the University of Virginia. What he desired above all was a discharge from the Army and permission from his father to embark on a literary career. But he knew that there was no hope of obtaining this permission. Since he knew also that Mr. Allan would not allow him to return to the university, there remained only one alternative. In his letters he brought up the subject of obtaining an appointment as a cadet to West Point. If he had to remain in the Army, the career of an officer, with the chance to rise to the highest ranks, was far preferable to the life of an enlisted man.

On January 1, 1829, with his regiment quartered at Fortress Monroe, Virginia, Edgar received notice of his promotion to sergeant major. This provided ample evidence that he could be a dependable and efficient soldier. But his Army success was of little concern to him; he waited anxiously for some news that his father was willing to help him get a discharge. A request by a person as wealthy and as influential as Mr. Allan could not be overlooked. Beyond this, all that was required was the payment of a small sum of money to the man who agreed to replace Edgar.

But all these hopes were to be temporarily suspended. On March 1st, Edgar received shocking news: his foster-mother, Mrs. Frances Allan, had died. The woman who had taken him into the Allan home out of love and pity and had defended him with all her strength against the bitter reproaches of his father, would never come to his aid again. Edgar had loved her dearly, and her love was all that deadened the pain of the rejection and the loneliness that he often felt. With her gone, he could truly say, as he later wrote, "I have no father—nor mother."

In her last hours, did Mrs. Allan reflect in agony over the future of the orphan boy she had tried so hard to make her husband accept as his own son? It appears that she continued to implore Mr. Allan to treat Edgar kindly for her sake. There is a touching story that, after realizing that her son would not arrive before she died, Frances Allan made her husband promise that she would not be buried until Edgar had a chance to see her for the last time.

Granted a ten-day furlough, Edgar hurried home to Richmond. But John Allan's summons had been sent too late. Frances Allan died on February 28th, and Edgar reached home on March 3rd, the day after the funeral. The tragedy, and the moment when he stood at his mother's grave in Shockoe Cemetery, must have affected Edgar deeply. An extremely sensitive boy, he had already shown a tendency toward quick depression and gloom. In the Allan household, once past his early childhood, he had become aware of not belonging, of the fact that as an orphan, not even legally adopted, he was different from his friends, secure in their family circles. Edgar had grasped eagerly after the two loves he needed—a mother love and an ideal love. Now, within the same cemetery, the two women, Mrs. Jane Stanard and Mrs. Allan, lay buried, and with them all the moments of warmth and acceptance that for Edgar would never return.

The death of Mrs. Allan seemed to soften his father's harsh attitude. When Edgar left Richmond on March 9th, the two were friendlier and an agreement had been reached. John Allan would help his son get an Army discharge and would use his influence to obtain an appointment to West Point. A substitute was found, and on April 15, 1829, Edgar received his official discharge.

It is evident that Edgar had few illusions about the reconciliation with his father. Mr. Allan's interest in placing him at West Point was simply an expedient to get him out of the house and into a permanent career. The Army, Allan believed, would control his son's erratic nature. In addition, he would be relieved of further responsibility.

Edgar's understanding of Mr. Allan was revealed in a letter he later wrote to his father. In reflecting on his mother's death, Edgar said, "If she had not have died while I was away there would have been nothing for me to regret. Your love I never valued—but she I believed loved me as her own child."

In May, Edgar went to Washington with letters of recommendation supplied by the officers at Fortress Monroe. They were all generous in their praise of the young soldier, speaking of "duties promptly and faithfully done," and of one whose "education is of a very high order" and who "appears to be free from bad habits." His first lieutenant maintained, in recommending Edgar, that "His habits are good and *entirely free from drinking.*"

As part of his application for entrance to West Point, Edgar presented these letters to Major John Eaton, Secretary of War. Meanwhile, Colonel James P. Preston, whose son had been Edgar's close friend and schoolmate in Richmond, wrote an enthusiastic letter to the Secretary of War:

. . . I know Mr. Poe and am acquainted with the fact of his having been born under circumstances of great adversity. I also know from his own productions and other undoubted proofs that he is a young gentleman *of genius and taleants.* I believe he is destined to be distinguished, since he has already gained reputation for taleants and attainements at the University of Virginia. I think him possessed of feeling and character peculiarly intitling him to public patronage.

Colonel Preston, a family friend, was convinced of Edgar's genius, "taleants," and "attainements." But John Allan, in whose home the young genius had lived for more than sixteen years, had no faith in his son's creative talents. With his other letters, Edgar carried one from his father, addressed to the Secretary of War. Mr. Allan offered a severe appraisal of his son, mixing blame and curt details with some grudging praise:

. . . He left me in consequence of some gambling at the University at Charlottesville, because (I presume) I refused to sanction a rule that the shopkeepers and others had adopted there, making Debts of Honours of all indiscretions. I have much pleasure in asserting that he stood his examination at the close of the year with great credit to himself. . . . Frankly, Sir, do I declare that he is no relation to me whatever; that I have many whom I have taken an active interest to promote theirs; with no other feeling than that, every man is my care, if he be in distress. . . .

John Allan went on to say that he asked nothing for himself, but hoped that the Secretary would aid Edgar in his future prospects. His blunt statement that Edgar was "no relation . . . whatever" gave clear indication of what treatment Edgar might expect in the future. Certainly, there was little chance of Edgar's inheriting his father's wealth.

Soon after presenting his West Point application, Edgar went to Baltimore to wait for the Secretary's decision. Bitter days of youthful sorrow, disappointment, and failure lay behind him. The achievement of manhood awaited him, but with it would come more intense struggles and frustrations.

6 · *West Point and the Creative Decision*

In Baltimore, Edgar waited impatiently for the expected West Point appointment. Upon first arriving, Edgar had shown his poem *Al Aaraaf* to William Wirt, a well-known lawyer and author whom he had met in Richmond. At Wirt's suggestion, Edgar next proceeded to the publishing firm of Carey, Lea and Carey in Philadelphia, leaving his manuscript there. It soon appeared that there was little chance of the firm's publishing a work by an unknown author unless they were guaranteed against all loss. In a letter to his father, Edgar urged him to back the publication, and pointed out that the limit of his loss would be $100 at the most, "supposing not a single copy of the work to be sold." Edgar maintained confidently that "It is more than probable that the work will be profitable & that I may gain instead of lose, even in a pecuniary way." Mr. Allan's reply was a prompt, curt refusal to aid in any manner.

The weeks passed with no news of the appointment. Again, Edgar was forced to send appealing letters to Mr. Allan for funds; and once more he was dependent on the grudging amounts sent by his father. The money was accompanied by the usual scolding, complaints, and warnings about spending too freely. By midsummer, Edgar began to despair of ever hearing from the War Department. In desperation, on July 23rd, he decided to make the trip to Washington once again. Unwilling to use part of his small store of money, Edgar had no choice but to travel on foot, both up and back, between Baltimore and Washington.

It was a wasted journey. From Secretary Eaton he learned that he could hope for an appointment only after those on the present list had been assigned. Ten cadets had priority over Edgar, and the earliest possibility for West Point entrance was vaguely set as some time between September, 1829, and the next year.

For Edgar, the months of anxious waiting and the necessity to guard every penny he received from his father made his existence almost unbearable. But in Baltimore new associations helped carry Edgar through one of the most discouraging periods he had ever faced. The city was the home of his relatives. The heroic General David Poe, his grandfather, who had led American patriots in driving the British out of Maryland during the Revolutionary War, was still remembered and respected. He had died in 1816, but his widow, Edgar's grandmother, and Mrs. Maria Clemm, his aunt, still lived in Baltimore.

One day in August, Edgar walked slowly up the stairs of a two-story house in Mechanics Row, Wilks Street. He carried his few possessions with him in a small bundle. His mood was a gloomy one; with his money almost gone and little hope of obtaining more, he was forced to leave his lodgings and move into an already overcrowded house.

As he climbed to the second floor, he felt somewhat cheered by the thought of the welcome he was certain to receive. He had visited there when he first arrived in Baltimore. In spite of the extreme poverty in which his aunt and grandmother lived, he had been made to feel that their home was his for as long as he wanted to stay.

When he knocked, the door was opened by a small, brown-haired girl who cried, "Eddie!" and jumped up and down in excitement. She was his seven-year-old cousin, Virginia. She put an arm around his waist and he pressed her to him affectionately.

His Aunt Maria came to the door smiling, and bent over to kiss him. "We're so happy to see you, Eddie," she said. She noticed the bundle under his arm. "Have you come to stay for a while?"

Edgar nodded. "I hope you don't mind. I know you're crowded. But it'll only be for a short time—until I get my appointment."

"Oh, Eddie, you needn't apologize," said his aunt. "There's always room for another."

Inside the front room he walked over to kiss his grandmother. The aged woman, almost completely paralyzed, sat in her chair smiling and nodding at him. Since the death of her husband, Mrs. Poe had lived with the Clemms. Because of the small pension she received from the government, the seventy-three-year-old widow of the distinguished General Poe was not entirely a burden to Edgar's Aunt Maria. At times the meager dole from the government was the family's only income.

As they chatted, Edgar heard the sound of footsteps coming from the attic, and soon he saw a thin, pale young man whose eyes seemed set in deep black hollows. His hair was long and uncombed and his clothes dirty and wrinkled.

"Welcome to our happy home," he said, with a deep bow. He spoke in a tone of pretended gayety, but beneath his words and careless smile Edgar could sense an emotion that bordered upon despair or hopelessness.

"Henry!" Edgar cried, holding out a hand. "How are you?"

As Henry grasped his hand, Edgar was concerned at his brother's unsteadiness and the tremor that ran through his body. "Aren't you feeling well?" he asked anxiously.

Henry seemed very tired as he dropped heavily into a chair. "Oh, I'll be all right," he said.

Glancing away, Edgar caught the disturbed look in his aunt's eyes. His brother, only twenty-two years old, had been in poor health for some time. His illness, described as the "wasting sickness," was actually tuberculosis. Edgar had known that Henry was ill, but now, gazing at his brother's haggard face and noticing how thin and slight his body was, he felt shocked. Could this be the same carefree boy who had visited him in Richmond just four years earlier—the boy who wore a naval uniform and talked eagerly of journeys to foreign lands?

Edgar knew that his aunt's worried look signified something beyond Henry's illness. In past years he recalled that his brother had found drinking an almost irresistible temptation. Because of his ill health and the physical weakness it produced, Henry had turned more and more to liquor until it controlled him completely. In a letter he wrote to his father, Edgar commented sadly,

. . . My grandmother is extremely poor & ill (paralytic). My aunt Maria if possible still worse & Henry entirely given up to drink & unable to help himself, much less me—

To this unfortunate household, already crowded and filled with misery, was now added another unhappy tenant. At times it must have seemed to Edgar that his future was as uncertain as that of the people around him. The entire family income was sufficient to supply only the most limited necessities. Another "Henry," young Henry Clemm, Aunt Maria's son, worked as a stonemason's apprentice. She tried to make a little money by taking in sewing. On these earnings and Grandmother Poe's small pension the family somehow managed.

When bedtime arrived, Edgar climbed upstairs to the attic where he and his brother would sleep. Henry's agony of restlessness, his coughing and pain, allowed little sleep for Edgar. He talked to Henry to try to soothe him, and wiped the perspiration from his face.

For Edgar the Clemm home was used as temporary quarters only. Repeated pleas to his father brought small sums of money irregularly, sufficient to pay for board and lodging elsewhere. But, in spite of all these hardships, he continued his writing and his attempts to contact a publisher. The creative urge, the thrill of shaping words into strange, beautiful phrases, burned so strongly inside him that he could not have stopped writing. Along with this was a new feeling of confidence that had come to him in Baltimore. He believed with an inspired certainty that his poem *Al Aaraaf* would find a publisher.

His confidence and persistence were bound to bring results. Earlier he had made the acquaintance of John Neal, publisher of the magazine, *The Yankee and Boston Literary Gazette*. To Neal, a distinguished critic whose opinions carried much weight, Edgar sent some samples of his poems. In September, 1829, came the exciting moment when he opened a copy of *The Yankee* to stare at the comment about a certain "E. A. P." Although critical of the poetry, Neal had offered some hopeful praise:

If E. A. P. of Baltimore—whose lines about "Heaven" though he professes to regard them as altogether superior to anything in the whole range of American poetry, save two or three trifles referred to, are, though nonsense, rather exquisite nonsense—would do himself justice he might make a beautiful and perhaps magnificent poem. There is a good deal here to justify such a hope.

This short paragraph of praise sent Edgar's spirits soaring into the clouds. But more important success was on its way. In November, the firm of Hatch & Dunning, Baltimore publishers, agreed to publish his poems.

Edgar wrote proudly to his father, "The Poems will be printed by Hatch & Dunning of this city upon terms advantageous to me they printing it & giving me 250 copies of the book:—I will send it on by Mr. Dunning who is going immediately to Richmond—"

Actually, Hatch & Dunning contracted to publish a collection titled, *Al Aaraaf, Tamerlane, and Minor Poems*. While the proofs were being prepared, Edgar sent some of the poems to various magazine editors, including John Neal. In December, 1829, Neal, again generous to the young poet, wrote:

The following passages are from the manuscript-works of a young author, about to be published in Baltimore. He is entirely a stranger to us, but with all their faults, if the remainder of "Al Aaraaf" and "Tamerlane" are as good as the body of the extracts here given—to say nothing of the more extraordinary parts, he will deserve to stand high—very high—in the estimation of the shining brotherhood. . . .

In his letter to Neal, Edgar chose rich, fanciful words to describe himself:

"I am young—not yet twenty—*am* a poet—if deep worship of all beauty can make me one—and wish to be so in the more common meaning of the word. I would give the world to embody one half the ideas afloat in my imagination."

Edgar admitted candidly, "I am and have been, from my childhood, an idler. . . ."

Neal printed Edgar's entire four-page letter. About his poems Edgar explained that the greater part was written before he was fifteen. Neal's words of praise, according to Edgar, were "the very first words of encouragement I ever remember to have heard."

In parts of the letter, Edgar discussed the poems that were to be published. *"Al Aaraaf,"* he said, "has some good poetry, and much extravagance, which I have not had time to throw away."

Al Aaraaf was a long, complex poem with unusual thought and imagery; its interpretation was to prove mystifying to some of the critics. In explaining the theme, Edgar said,

Al Aaraaf is a tale of another world—the star discovered by Tycho Brahe, which appeared and disappeared so suddenly—or rather, it is no tale at all. I will insert an extract about the palace of its presiding Deity, in which you will see that I have supposed many of the lost sculptures of our world to have flown (in spirit) to the star *Al Aaraaf*— a delicate place, more suited to their divinity.

A description of the palace in which the Deity lived was then quoted from the poem:

> Uprear'd upon such height arose a pile
> Of gorgeous columns on th'unburthened air—
> Flashing, from Parian marble, that twin-smile
> Far down upon the wave that sparkled there.

In December, 1829, Edgar may have felt that all of the sacrifices of the past year—the days of loneliness, of going hungry, of living in fear and uncertainty—were of small concern, for in his hands he held a thin, blue-covered volume of poetry. Its title page read, *AL AARAAF, TAMERLANE and MINOR POEMS.* Beneath it were the magic words, *BY EDGAR A. POE.* No more would he have to remain an anonymous "Bostonian."

For its dedication, the seventy-two-page volume contained a line written by John Cleveland, the seventeenth-century poet:

> Who drinks the deepest?—here's to him.

Tamerlane, now in a revised form, was dedicated respectfully to John Neal. The nine minor poems included three which Edgar had also changed somewhat since their appearance in his Boston booklet. After a short paragraph in which he referred to the poems as "the crude compositions of my earliest boyhood," Edgar offered a *Sonnet—To Science* as his Preface, before launching into *Al Aaraaf*. In the sonnet, science becomes the poet's enemy, destroying the world of beauty and imagination by prying and classifying:

> Science! true daughter of Old Time thou art!
> Who alterest all things with thy peering eyes.
> Why preyest thou thus upon the poet's heart,
> Vulture, whose wings are dull realities?

This criticism came from a young man who was later to demonstrate an astonishing knowledge of science and the scientific approach in his detective stories; his skill with cryptograms (as in *The Gold Bug*); his background in astronomy, revealed in *Hans Pfaall,* and *The Balloon-Hoax;* and his brilliance in deduction, as shown in *Maelzel's Chess-Player.* Throughout his life Edgar was to display the double genius of one who could travel from the poet's strange world of fantasy to the precise, logical, and even mathematical world of the scientist.

Soon after the publication of his poems, Edgar returned to Richmond. Impressed by the recognition given his son, Mr. Allan now adopted a friendlier attitude toward him, suggesting that he wait at home for his appointment. The new year began with Edgar back in familiar surroundings, resuming Richmond friendships and visiting with the Mackenzies and with his sister, Rosalie. Life in the Allan home, with its luxurious furnishings, servants, and well-prepared food, must have served as a painful reminder to Edgar of the sufferings he had just endured. As he wandered about the large home, deeper and more painful memories must have haunted him. The objects he saw and touched were certain to remind him of his dead foster-mother. And did remembered streets and houses in Richmond bring back the anguish of Elmira and Mrs. Stanard? He didn't let go of memories easily. The images of his lost loves were concealed in the shadows of his mind, ready to return and torment him.

Watching his father's sufferings as he moved about on his lame foot, Edgar realized that Mr. Allan's health had grown worse. The fifty-year-old man seemed to have aged beyond his years and to have lost much of his vigor. But, as the weeks passed, it also became apparent that his antagonism toward Edgar, his anger over his son's behavior at the university, had not changed. His irritation and resentment lay close to the surface and flared forth often.

A deeper, more delicate hostility existed between the two—one that Edgar had difficulty in suppressing. It was based on the private behavior of John Allan in his relations with women. Years before, Edgar had been aware that his father was not faithful to his mother. The nature of Mr. Allan's associations with women outside of his home had been clear to both Edgar and Mrs. Allan. Edgar resented his father's behavior, and on occasion had more than hinted at this resentment. John Allan was not one to take even implied criticism from an orphan boy whose actions had already irked him. While Edgar could not be aware of all the details, his father's unfaithfulness to his wife seems evident in the statements made in Mr. Allan's will. On December 31, 1832, Allan placed definite instructions in writing:

I desire that my executors shall out of my estate provide give to ———————— a good english education for two boys sons of Mrs. Elizabeth Wills, which she says are mine, I do not know their names, but the remaining fifth, four parts of which I have disposed of must go in equal shares to them or the survivor of them . . .

Some time in March, 1830, Edgar received notice of his appointment to West Point. The months spent at home had been far from comfortable and he may have had little regret in leaving. But perhaps there were moments of sadness in saying goodbye to his Aunt Nancy, his sister, and his Richmond friends. His regrets might have been deeper if he could have foreseen the future: not only was the Allan home closed to him forever as a permanent refuge, but he would never again be welcome inside its doors.

Entrance examinations were scheduled for June, and in mid-May Edgar left to board a steamboat; his first stop would be Baltimore, and from there he would proceed to West Point. John Allan accompanied him to the boat. Some of the old affection they once shared may have touched father and son momentarily. As he shook hands with the older man, Edgar's thoughts were gloomy. He believed, as he wrote later, that in parting from his father he would never see him again.

At Baltimore, Edgar visited with the Clemms, and by the last week in June he was present at West Point, where he took his entrance examinations. These he passed with little difficulty; consequently, on July 1, 1830, Edgar took the required oath of allegiance, becoming Cadet Edgar Poe, whose duties and classes started at sunrise and did not end until nine-thirty at night.

Edgar and two roommates, Thomas W. Gibson and Timothy Pickering Jones, were assigned to 28 South Barracks. From the start Edgar had little interest in a military career; his taste of Army life had already filled him with a dislike of its rigid routine and constant emphasis upon physical fitness. He had planned to complete the West Point course in six months, believing that his education and previous Army experience would make this possible. But he had now reached a point where the urge to create was all that mattered; within his mind the rich images of his world of fantasy and the brilliant ideas of a real world demanded expression. With each day his rebellion against a life of drills and inspections grew stronger. As in the past, John Allan's reluctance to provide him with needed money made his situation even worse. Edgar was given his Army pay and rations, but, unlike the majority of the cadets, he received no allowance from home.

The unbroken sequence of classes, drill, and study made West Point far more monotonous to Edgar than the Army days he had experienced at Fort Moultrie. There the routine duties were brief and he had had ample time to explore Sullivan's Island, or to dream and create. At West Point, with its exhausting routine, he was granted only a few precious hours for writing.

In these depressing surroundings he turned again to drink. There are accounts of how he or his roommates slipped out of Room 28 to purchase bottles of brandy. These were drunk late at night, after "lights out." But Edgar's behavior seemed to follow the usual pattern of young soldiers who drink occasionally to escape the boring sameness of military life. He could not have drunk regularly, even if he had wanted to, since he had neither the money nor the credit.

Years later Thomas Gibson, his roommate, commented on Edgar's appearance and attitude:

Poe at that time, though only twenty years of age, had the appearance of being much older. He had a worn, weary discontented look, not easily forgotten by those who were intimate with him. Poe was easily fretted by any jest at his expense. . . .

The studies of the Academy, Poe utterly ignored. I doubt if he ever studied a page of Lacroix, unless it was to glance hastily over it in the lecture room, while others of his section were reciting. It was evident from the first that he had no intention of going through with the course. . . .

Beginning in October, 1830, a series of events combined to drive Edgar into complete rebellion against West Point and a career he had never wanted. His letters to Mr. Allan remained unanswered, and it was only indirectly that he heard the astonishing news: his father had re-married. For some time John Allan had been paying court to Miss Louisa Gabriella Patterson, an attractive New York woman who was visiting in Richmond. On October 5th, she became his second wife. To Edgar, frustrated and miserable, his creative dreams buried under the deadly monotony of Army routine, Mr. Allan's marriage foretold the end of anything he had hoped to retain from the past. His greatest need had been one of belonging—of having permanent ties. Although he had remarked earlier, with bitterness, that he had "no father—nor mother," he still addressed letters to Mr. Allan as "Dear Pa," clutching at a hope that somehow the old bond of affection would never be completely broken. His father's farewell at the boat, firm and final, had signaled an end to the past; and now the presence of a strange woman at home meant that he was truly adrift—without ties, unwanted.

Late in 1830, as the result of a letter received by John Allan from Sergeant Samuel "Bully" Graves, the soldier who had been paid to replace Edgar at Fortress Monroe, a serious quarrel broke out between father and son. In claiming that Edgar owed him money, which he had attempted previously to collect, Graves referred to an insulting remark made by Edgar about his father. The nature of the debt to Graves was not clear. Either Edgar had agreed to pay the sergeant an extra amount of money for replacing him, and concealed this arrangement from his father, or Edgar may have simply borrowed money from Graves, neglecting to repay it. Allan, furiously angry, believed that Edgar had spent the money that he, his father, had sent him for a replacement. Allan now paid Graves' claim and informed Edgar that he was "banished from his affections" and should discontinue all communication.

On January 3, 1831, Edgar replied with a long, accusing letter:

I suppose, (altho' you desire no further communication with yourself, on my part,) that your restriction does not extend to my answering your final letter.

Edgar made bitter reference to what he knew to be true—that at the time the Allans had taken him into their home, his grandfather, General David Poe, had been eager to shelter him, but had yielded to the pleas of Mrs. Allan, who had fallen in love with the young child. Edgar turned back the clock to the year 1811, when fate had almost conspired to place him, as an infant, in the Allan home. In brooding over the choice that might have been made, he hurled a fierce accusation at Allan:

Did I, when an infant, sollicit your charity and protection, or was it of your own free will, that you volunteered your services in my behalf? It is well known to respectable individuals in Baltimore, and elsewhere, that my Grandfather (my natural protector at the time you interposed) was wealthy, and that I was his favourite grand-child— But the promises of adoption, and liberal education which you held forth to him in a letter which is now in possession of my family, induced him to resign all care of me into your hands.

Edgar then makes it plain that he has reached a point of desperation:

You sent me to West Point like a beggar. The same difficulties are threatening me as before at Charlottesville—and I must resign.

In gloomy reference to his future life, "which thank God will not endure long," Edgar predicts that his years will be passed in "indigence and sickness." He asks that Allan, as his guardian, should send him written permission to leave West Point, reminding his father that in any case he intends to leave without permission. Edgar closes, announcing,

From the time of writing this I shall neglect my studies and duties at the institution—if I do not receive your answer in 10 days—I will leave the point without—for otherwise I should subject myself to dismission.

To this letter of fierce rebellion, John Allan had no intention of replying. He merely wrote on the letter, "I recd this on the 10th & did not from its conclusion deem it necessary to reply. . . . I do not think the Boy has one good quality. He may do or act as he pleases, thou' I wd have saved him but on his own terms & conditions since I cannot believe a word he writes. His letter is the most barefaced one-sided statement."

The dreary days at West Point were soon to be ended. But, although West Point had meant the stifling of much of Edgar's creative talent, even its rigid, unimaginative atmosphere could not prevent the light of his genius from finally streaming through. In an earlier note to his father, Edgar commented that he had met General Scott and that he was "very much pleased with Colonel Thayer." It appears that Colonel Sylvanus Thayer, upon hearing of Edgar's poetic ability, had chatted with him for a time, inquiring with interest about his poems. Later, a summons was received at the barracks for Cadet Edgar Poe to report to Colonel Thayer—and to bring his manuscripts.

Once he was instructed to be "at ease" before the Colonel, the two began an animated discussion of Edgar's writings. Later, the Colonel leafed through the manuscript, noticing the colorful titles: *To Helen, The Valley of Nis, The Doomed City*. . . .

"*The Valley of Nis*," the Colonel said, smiling. "What kind of a valley is that?"

"Nis," Edgar explained, "is 'sin,' inverted."

"Of course," said Colonel Thayer. He read on silently, commenting after a while, "Indeed, a valley of restlessness." He had noted the lines,

> *Now* each visitor shall confess,
> The sad valley's restlessness.
> Nothing there is motionless—
> Nothing save the airs that brood
> Over the magic solitude.

"And *The Doomed City*," the Colonel repeated, as he turned a page. He read the first few lines and glanced quickly at Edgar, his eyes curious. What kind of strange young man was this who wrote such gloomy, morbid poetry?

> Lo! Death has reared himself a throne
> In a strange city lying alone
> Far down within the dim West,
> Where the good and the bad, and the worst and the best,
> Have gone to their eternal rest.

The doomed city where death reigns receives "no rays from the Holy Heaven . . ." Instead, "light from out the lurid sea streams up . . ." It ascends past turrets, pinnacles, domes, spires—then gleaming,

> Up many and many a marvellous shrine
> Whose wreathed frizes intertwine
> The viol, the violet, and the vine.

The city with its "resigned" and "melancholy" waters lies "hideously serene,"

> While from a proud tower in town
> Death looks gigantically down.

In picturing its inevitable doom, Edgar wrote,

> And when, amid no earthly moans,
> Down, down that town shall settle hence,
> Hell, rising from a thousand thrones,
> Shall do it reverence.

The Colonel scanned other poems, *The Paean, Irene,* and *Israfel.* "Who is Israfel?" he asked.

"He is the angel Israfel, described in the *Koran,*" Edgar explained. "His heart-strings are a lute, and he has the sweetest voice of all God's creatures."

Colonel Thayer folded the manuscript. "You have unusual ability in writing," he said. "Have you thought of having your poems published?"

Edgar nodded eagerly. "I have thought of it often."

The Colonel smiled at him. "I understand the cadets think highly of your writings. If the poems were published, I'm sure they would be happy to purchase copies."

Colonel Thayer's encouragement prompted Edgar to propose a plan that had occurred to him. "With your permission, sir," he said, "I would like to circulate a subscription list among the cadets. Such a list would aid me in having the poems published."

"An excellent idea," said the Colonel. "Permission is granted."

The cadets did subscribe, agreeing to pay seventy-five cents for the volume of poetry, and in this way guaranteeing Edgar an advance sale of almost two hundred copies. Edgar wrote at once to Elam Bliss, a New York publisher, who came to West Point to discuss plans for publication. When Bliss left, Edgar was in a state of elation; the promise had been made—the second edition of his poems was certain to appear.

But as satisfying as this success was, it could not change Edgar's determination to leave West Point. He intended to carry out the angry pledge he had made to his father: he would leave with or without permission. Since he received no response from Mr. Allan, he proceeded with his scheme to neglect all studies and duties. During the month of January, 1831, Edgar violated military regulations, staying away from drills, formations, classes, and church, and deliberately ignored any orders he received.

On January 28th, at a general court-martial, Cadet Edgar Allan Poe was charged with "Gross Neglect of Duty," and "Disobedience of Orders." On the first charge he was accused of absenting himself from "all Academical duties between the 15th and 27th January

1831 . . ." The second charge was that he had failed to attend church when ordered to do so by the Officer of the Day.

After pleading "not guilty" to a charge that he had absented himself from certain parades and roll calls, Edgar pleaded "guilty" to all the other charges. He was found guilty by the court and his dismissal from West Point ordered. The date for dismissal was set for March 6, 1831, but Edgar, in a highly nervous state, could see no reason for wasting further time at West Point. He was torn by powerful, conflicting emotions—depressed by the final break with his father and by the uncertainty of his future, and yet eager to get to New York where he could wait for his poems to appear in print.

The combination of all these worries and fears became too much for him to carry, and on February 19th, when he left the Academy, he was seriously ill. From New York, two days later, he wrote an anguished letter to John Allan. In it are the first indications that his health is starting to break down. He says, "The whole academy have interested themselves in my behalf because my only crime was being *sick*. . . ." Because of illness, or delicate health, he could no longer endure the rigid military discipline and training with its rough physical demands.

He writes accusingly to his father, ". . . if you had granted me permission to resign—all might have been avoided. I have not strength nor energy left to write what I feel. . . . You one day or other will feel how you have treated me. . . . I have caught a most violent cold and am confined to my bed—I have no money—no friends— I have written to my brother—but he cannot help me . . . besides a most violent cold on my lungs my *ear* discharges blood and matter continually and my headache is distracting. . . ."

Again, in spite of all intentions, he was forced to beg in humiliation, "Please send me a little money—quickly—and forget what I said about you— God bless you."

From John Allan came neither money nor a response. But a week later Edgar recovered sufficiently to leave his room and walk to the office of Elam Bliss, the publisher, at 111 Broadway.

In April, 1831, a volume of 124 pages, bound in green covers, appeared in New York City. The title page contained the simple heading, POEMS by EDGAR ALLAN POE. In gratitude Edgar had written,

TO THE U.S. CORPS OF CADETS
THIS VOLUME IS
RESPECTFULLY DEDICATED

The second edition of his poems, which cadets at West Point would soon be reading, contained eleven of his most famous poems, plus revisions of *Tamerlane* and *Al Aaraaf*. It appears that much of this new poetry had been composed at home while waiting for the appointment to the Academy. Included was his poem *To Helen,* produced reverently in homage to Jane Stanard, the ideal woman who had given a young boy love and understanding.

Publication of a volume of poetry by a young, unknown poet made little impression upon New York literary circles. Certainly, the dreams of recognition, if there were any, vanished abruptly. Now, with the Richmond home barred to him, the road led again to the only place where he was welcome—with his Aunt Maria in Baltimore. The same desperate, hand-to-mouth existence awaited him as he moved into the crowded rooms. But there was one evident change: his brother Henry was dying.

As Edgar sat in the small attic room, with the heat of the summer sun turning the air witheringly hot, he must have been filled with deep despair. His life so far had been a series of unhappy, tragic circumstances; none of his plans had worked out, and his dreams had only led to frustration. Now, in the last weeks of Henry's feverish breathing and coughing, he must sit by his brother's wasted form and watch his life slip away. On Tuesday, August 2, 1831, a simple announcement appeared in the *Baltimore American:*

Died last evening W. H. Poe, aged 24 years. His friends and acquaintances are invited to attend his funeral this morning at 9, from the dwelling of Mrs. Clemm in Wilks Street.

During his long illness, Henry had incurred bills for medical care for which Edgar had signed a note. The debt was eighty dollars, and soon after Henry's death demands were made upon Edgar for payment. Failure to pay a debt could mean long imprisonment. Once more he appealed to John Allan in a series of pleading letters. In November, 1831, to the man he still addressed as "My dear Pa," he wrote,

. . . I was arrested eleven days ago for a debt which I never expected to have to pay, and which was incurred as much on Henry's account as on my own about two years ago. I would rather have done any thing on earth than apply to you again after your late kindness—but indeed I have no other resource, and I am in bad health, and unable to undergo as much hardships as formerly or I never would have asked you to give me another cent.

Not hearing from his father, Edgar wrote imploringly a month later to beg for Mr. Allan's aid. But the imprisonment, which first appeared imminent, was somehow avoided. Whether the debt was paid or not has never been revealed. Some time after the emergency, it appears that John Allan had written instructions to John Walsh, a Baltimore business associate, to see that Edgar was freed from prison and given "$20 besides to keep him out of further difficulties . . ."

December, 1831, signaled the end of another year of painful struggle for a young man about to turn twenty-two. Perhaps the knowledge that John Allan still cared enough to come to his rescue may have given Edgar a touch of cheer and hope as the new year entered. With the death of Henry he now lived alone in his aunt's attic, sharing a starvation diet with her, young Henry Clemm, Virginia, and his grandmother. But in the year 1832 he was to start the slow climb to success, turning his brilliant, fantastic imagination to a new field. Rejection, baffled hopes, the steady deterioration of his health—none of these could stop the sweep of a magic pen that painted characters and plots in a strange world that no writer had ever before entered.

7 · *The Broken Ties, and a Hint of Success*

THE young man seated at a small table in the attic leaned back with a sigh and put his pen down. He was exhausted, and the lines of heavy black ink that twisted irregularly across the sheets of paper floated and blurred before his eyes. But the tiredness could not subdue his elation; all that mattered was that the last line lay boldly written on the page. The short story was completed. In the bizarre tale of *Metzengerstein,* an evil young nobleman guilty of "shameful debaucheries—flagrant treacheries—unheard of atrocities," Edgar had created a shocking story of terror and death. Never before had a writer conceived of a character so strange and of happenings that rose to so fearful a climax!

84

Bitter hatred between two powerful families, the Berlifitzings and Metzengersteins, is the story's opening theme. Young Frederick, Baron Metzengerstein, who has inherited the family's vast possessions, is a man whose evil nature and passion for revenge are beyond control. Within the first three days of his inheritance he has committed appalling crimes, and now he adds one more to the list:

On the night of the fourth day, the stables of the Castle Berlifitzing were discovered to be on fire; and the unanimous opinion of the neighborhood added the crime of the incendiary to the already hideous list of the Baron's misdemeanors and enormities.

Seated alone in an upper apartment of the family palace, the Baron, completely indifferent to the flaming stables of his neighbor, is staring at the faded tapestry hangings which swing upon the ancient walls. His eyes are turned to the figure of an "enormous, and unnaturally colored horse, represented in the tapestry as belonging to a Saracen ancestor of the family of his rival. The horse itself, in the foreground of the design, stood motionless and statue-like—while, farther back, its discomfited rider perished by the dagger of a Metzengerstein."

After turning his gaze away momentarily, the Baron glances again at the horse in the tapestry. "To his extreme horror and astonishment, the head of the gigantic steed had, in the meantime, altered its position. The neck of the animal, before arched, as if in compassion, over the prostrate body of its lord, was now extended, at full length, in the direction of the Baron."

Soon a "gigantic and fiery-colored" horse, apparently owned by no one, appears at the palace. It had been caught "flying, all smoking and foaming with rage, from the burning stables of the Castle Berlifitzing."

At the story's amazing ending, the Baron, who has spent his days "riveted to the saddle of that colossal horse," now finds it carrying him toward his own "crackling . . . rocking," fiercely burning palace. He has time for only a "solitary shriek," and then,

One instant, and the clattering of hoofs resounded sharply and shrilly above the roaring of the flames and the shrieking of the winds—another, and, clearing at a single plunge the gate-way and the moat, the steed bounded far up the tottering staircases of the palace, and, with its rider, disappeared amid the whirlwind of chaotic fire.

Before the end of 1831, in an amazing illustration of his versatility, Edgar wrote five stories in varying styles, ranging from the bizarre to the satirically humorous. On June 4th, he had picked up the *Philadelphia Saturday Courier,* and a boldfaced announcement caught his eye:

A PRIZE CONTEST . . . THE COURIER OFFERS ONE HUNDRED DOLLARS FOR THE BEST SHORT STORY . . . STORIES MUST BE SUBMITTED BY DECEMBER 1, 1831 . . .

To the half-starved family, the sum of $100 was almost too great to dream about; it could pay the food bill for weeks to come. Edgar submitted his five stories in the contest. But when the winning story was announced on December 31, 1831, it was plain that the judges did not rate Edgar's bizarre tales very highly. *Love's Martyr,* a sentimental story by Delia S. Bacon, was awarded the prize. The *Courier* contest brought no money into the Clemm household; it was another of the bitter disappointments that Edgar had learned to expect and to suffer.

The judges may not have recognized the unusual qualities of his stories, but the editors did. *Metzengerstein* was published in the *Courier* on January 14, 1832, and the remaining four stories appeared in succeeding months. Edgar received no pay for these, but the fact that the editors had chosen to print his first stories encouraged him to continue experimenting in this new field. The themes that fascinated him—those that appeared in his earliest poems—remained unchanged. He wrote always about love, ideal and eternal, and about beauty and death. Perhaps because his thoughts returned constantly to Mrs. Stanard and Mrs. Allan, he wrote of what he believed to be the supreme tragedy—the death of a beautiful woman.

Edgar's genius allowed him to see beyond the forms created by other men—to see things differently and with the fresh touch of originality. He was bound to become an innovator. His imagination gave the short story a new form, one that other writers had not visioned.

During the year 1832, only the fierce need to create could have kept him from collapsing. With his Aunt Maria, Virginia, and his grandmother he survived in poverty and misery beyond description. Perhaps a little aid came from his Baltimore relatives, a wealthy uncle and a cousin who lived nearby. But success in writing seemed beyond his reach. The stories he sent to magazines received favorable comment—nothing more. He had received no assistance from John Allan, and had not written to him for almost two years. Finally, in a moment of complete despair, he was forced to send his most desperate appeal to Allan. On April 12, 1833, he wrote,

It has now been more than two years since you have assisted me, and more than three since you have spoken to me. I feel little hope that you will pay any regard to this letter, but still I cannot refrain from making one more attempt to interest you in my behalf. If you will only consider in what a situation I am placed you will surely pity me—without friends, without any means, consequently of obtaining employment, I am perishing—absolutely perishing for want of aid. And yet I am not idle—nor addicted to any vice—nor have I committed any offense against society which would render me deserving of so hard a fate. For God's sake pity me, and save me from destruction.

There is no evidence that Allan replied to this plea, the last letter that Edgar wrote to his father. How Edgar and the Clemm family managed to live throughout the starvation years of 1832 and 1833 has never been determined. Some food and money must have been contributed by his uncle, Henry Herring, and a cousin, Neilson Poe. The records reveal little of Edgar's activities in those years. The presumption is that he worked part-time jobs of various types. But there is one certainty—he continued doggedly to write and revise his stories and to send them out to magazine editors. By May of 1833 he had completed eleven stories which were later to be titled *Tales of the Folio Club*.

One day Edgar turned the pages of the *Baltimore Saturday Visiter* and his eye was caught by an unusual announcement. It was headed "Premiums," and went on to explain,

The proprietors of the *Baltimore Saturday Visiter* feeling desirous of encouraging literature, and at the same time serving their readers with the best that lies within their reach, offer a premium of 50 dollars for the best Tale and 25 dollars for the best Poem, not exceeding one hundred lines, that shall be offered them between the present period and the first of October next.

As Edgar finished reading, his spirits soared. He felt that the stories he had written were better than his earlier ones, and that he now had a good chance of winning the fifty-dollar premium. The problem was to choose the tales to be submitted. Seated in his attic room, he spread out his manuscripts before him. He turned the pages of a story he believed to be one of his best. It carried the strange title: *A MS. Found in a Bottle*. Edgar scanned the first page and nodded his head in approval. In this tale he had turned again to the sea for an account of fearful happenings set in an atmosphere of the supernatural. "After many years spent in foreign travel," he wrote, "I sailed in the year 18—, from the port of Batavia, in the rich and populous island of Java, on a voyage to the Archipelago Islands. I went as passenger—having no other inducement than a kind of nervous restlessness which haunted me as a fiend."

After a voyage of many days he became aware of a strange cloud on the horizon. "The air now became intolerably hot . . ." and "every breath of wind died away . . ." In this calm he felt a presentiment of evil: "Indeed every appearance warranted me in apprehending a Simoon." Soon the ship began quivering and the Simoon, a whirling funnel of wind and water, descended upon the ship. "In the next instant a wilderness of foam hurled us upon our beam-ends, and, rushing over us fore and aft, swept the entire decks from stem to stern."

When the shattered ship had righted itself, he and an old Swede were the only two survivors. The ship, a mere hulk, was beyond their control and was driven along by violent winds. It careened through wild seas for five days.

Edgar wrote, "We waited in vain for the arrival of the sixth day —that day to me has not yet arrived—to the Swede never did arrive. Thenceforward we were enshrouded in pitchy darkness, so that we could not have seen an object at twenty paces from the ship."

In the midst of this eternal night, the ocean began to heave in mountainous billows. "At times we gasped for breath at an elevation beyond the albatross—at times became dizzy with the velocity of our descent into some watery hell, where the air grew stagnant, and no sound disturbed the slumbers of the kraken."

As the ship plunged downward he heard a terrible scream from his companion. Directly above them a gigantic ship, its "huge hull . . . of a deep dingy black," poised upon the summit of a wave. When it crashed down upon their vessel he found himself hurled into its rigging. He is now upon a derelict ghost ship, unseen and unnoticed by her ancient, ghastly crew.

He begins to keep a journal of the incredible events. "It is true that I may not find an opportunity of transmitting it to the world," he says, "but I will not fail to endeavor. At the last moment, I will enclose the MS. in a bottle, and cast it within the sea."

The MS. Found in a Bottle was one of a group of stories Edgar submitted in the contest. He had also decided to compete for the

$25 poetry prize, and his entry was titled *The Coliseum*. The days of waiting must have been filled with hours of doubt and agony. Luck had never shown a smiling face to him, and even though, in the brilliance and perception of his mind, he must have known that his stories were superior to those written by other American authors, the terrible disappointments of the past could not allow him to be exceedingly hopeful. Perhaps his spirits were kept up by his Aunt Maria, whose faith and optimism would always support him, and by his eleven-year-old cousin, Virginia, whose beautiful, laughing eyes could draw him out of bitter moods.

On October 12, 1833, the *Visiter* announced the judges' decision. The letter from the three judges, John P. Kennedy, J. H. B. Latrobe, and J. H. Miller, printed in the *Visiter,* was in itself the most glowing commendation any author could receive:

Of the tales submitted there were many of various and distinguished excellence; but the singular force and beauty of those offered by "The Tales of the Folio Club," it may be said without disparagement to the high merit of others presented in the competition, left us no ground for doubt in making choice of one from that collection. We have accordingly, awarded the prize in this department to the tale bearing the title of "A MS. Found in a Bottle."

Edgar had won the $50 prize! But the praise he received from the judges went far beyond the contents of the winning story. "It would scarcely be doing justice to the author of this collection to say the tale we have chosen is the best of the six offered by him," the judges commented. They insisted that "the writer owes it to his own reputation, as well as to the gratification of the community to publish the whole volume." Their enthusiasm about the stories, displayed in the adjectives they used, was more than enough to warm Edgar's heart. His *Tales of the Folio Club* were described as having a "wild, vigorous and poetical imagination, a rich style, a fertile invention, and varied and curious learning." They explained that the *MS. Found in a Bottle* had been chosen, *not* because of "any superior merit in its execution over the others by the same author," but rather because of "the originality of its conception and its length."

Edgar's poem, *The Coliseum,* did not win the $25 prize—the judges chose *Song of the Winds,* a poem by John H. Hewitt, the editor of the *Baltimore Saturday Visiter*. Still, they thought highly of *The Coliseum,* and it was scheduled for publication. On October

19, 1833, *A MS. Found in a Bottle* appeared in the *Visiter,* and the following week Edgar's poem was printed.

The Coliseum, written in blank verse, paints the greatness of "antique" Rome. Edgar pictured its broken ruins and decay:

> Here, where a hero fell, a column falls!
> Here, where the mimic eagle glared in the gold,
> A midnight vigil holds the swarthy bat!
> Here, where the dames of Rome their gilded hair
> Waved to the wind, now wave the reed and thistle!
> Here, where on golden throne the monarch lolled,
> Glides, spectre-like, unto his marble home,
> Lit by the wan light of the horned moon,
> The swift and silent lizard of the stones!

Are these ruins, he asks, all that remain—all that are left "By the corrosive Hours to Fate and me?" The Echoes answer, "Not all!" Much of ancient Rome will live eternally—its renown, wonder, mysteries, and memories.

Several days after the *Visiter's* announcement of his prize-winning story, Edgar decided to pay a visit to the judges. He made the acquaintance of John Pendleton Kennedy, a distinguished lawyer and novelist. Kennedy quickly realized that in Edgar the judges had discovered a writer of remarkable talent. The two became friends, and in succeeding months Kennedy helped Edgar in many ways.

On a Monday following the publication of *A MS. Found in a Bottle,* a young man walked into the office of J. H. B. Latrobe, one of the judges. Looking up from his desk, Latrobe noticed that his visitor was dressed entirely in black, with his frock coat buttoned to the throat, so that no touch of white could be seen.

The unusual, black-clothed figure bowed gravely and spoke in a soft voice: "I am Edgar Allan Poe, the writer of the winning tale. I came to thank you for honoring me with the award."

Latrobe accepted the thanks graciously, smiling, and motioning Edgar to a seat. He was an observant man and had already scanned Edgar's coat, hat, boots, and gloves, noting that they had seen their best days. But they were neat in every respect, well mended and carefully brushed.

"You should not at all be grateful to us," Latrobe said, smiling. "Your story deserved the award. In fact, we were unanimous in our agreement that all the *Folio Club Tales* were far superior to the others entered in the competition. We had great difficulty in choosing one best one out of so excellent a group."

The praise made Edgar's face glow with elation. He had waited long for some sign of recognition and a chance for success. The high value the judges had placed upon his entire group of stories now led him to hope that success was not too far away. He murmured his thanks to Latrobe.

"Are you now occupied with some new literary works?" Latrobe asked.

Edgar nodded. "Yes, I am," he said. His solemn face relaxed and a smile touched his lips. "I am embarked upon a voyage to the moon."

Latrobe's eyebrows lifted in surprise. "A voyage to the moon?" he questioned. "Is this a scientific work?"

Edgar smiled more broadly. "Both scientific and imaginary. It is about one Hans Pfaall who departs rather suddenly from Rotterdam—in a balloon!"

"I see," said Latrobe, with a laugh. "And of what is your balloon constructed?"

"Of cambric muslin," said Edgar. "It will receive three coats of varnish—and I am certain it will be quite as strong as silk and a good deal less expensive."

"What of the inflation?" Latrobe asked. "What type of gas will it contain?"

Edgar's eyes gleamed with amusement. "A secret type—never before used. It is a constituent of azote, long considered irreducible, and its density is about 37.4 times less than that of hydrogen." He went on with great eagerness to give all the details of the balloon's construction and to explain all the technical aspects of a flight into space with a knowledge and a certainty that astonished Latrobe. It seemed that he had planned every step of the voyage to the moon. He discussed the laws of gravity, the height of the earth's atmosphere, and the capacities of balloons. In describing the ascent, Edgar lost his solemn, restrained way of speaking. He began to speak rapidly, wave his hands about, and even clap his hands and stamp his foot when he wanted to emphasize a particularly exciting moment in the voyage. Latrobe, in fascination, was swept along with him on the imaginary journey through space.

Edgar finished his account of a balloon voyage, his face flushed and excited and his voice at a high pitch. He stopped abruptly and burst out laughing. "I must apologize," he said. "I was quite carried away . . . I don't usually become so excitable."

"Not at all," said Latrobe. "It isn't every day that one makes a balloon ascent to the moon! And I must say I thoroughly enjoyed making the voyage with you."

Latrobe never forgot the meeting, his impressions of Edgar, and the fascinating voyage to the moon. In an address given in 1877, he recalled many details of that unusual day:

Of this interview, the only one I ever had with Mr. Poe, my recollection is very distinct, indeed— He was if anything, below the middle size, and yet could not be described as a small man. His figure was remarkably good, and he carried himself erect and well, as one who had been trained to it. . . . On most men his clothes would have looked shabby and seedy, but there was something about this man that prevented one from criticizing his garments. . . .

About his features Latrobe remembered that "His forehead was high, and remarkable for the great development at the temple . . . The expression of his face was grave, almost sad, except when he became engaged in conversation, when it became animated and changeable."

During this period of concentration upon his stories, Edgar made the acquaintance of several members of the Baltimore literary circle. John H. Hewitt, the winner of the *Visiter's* poetry prize, became his friend, as did Lambert Wilmer, a newspaper writer.

In the late spring of 1833, the Clemm family moved to a small two-story building at Number 3 Amity Street, in the western section of Baltimore. Here they were more crowded than before, but Edgar still managed to write continuously, completing eleven of his *Tales of the Folio Club*. Later he sent these to the firm of Carey and Lea, in Philadelphia, but, in spite of the influence and endorsement of John Kennedy, the tales were not published. One of the stories, *Epimanes,* had been offered to the *New England Magazine* by Edgar in May, 1833, as part of a collection which was at that time titled *Eleven Tales of the Arabesque*. However, the editors showed no interest in the story.

The recognition he received as a result of winning the *Visiter's* contest provided only a first step toward success in the literary field. The financial return from his writings was still very small, and with the arrival of the new year the wretched, starving existence of the Clemm family remained unchanged. Early in 1834 Edgar found a new cause for worry. On several occasions, through his

Baltimore relatives, he had heard that John Allan's health was failing rapidly. Allan, now fifty-four, was suffering acutely from the dropsy. Because of the illness he was unable to lie down, and he spent his days and nights sitting upright in an armchair.

The news shocked Edgar and convinced him that he must see his foster-father at once, so he decided to make an unannounced visit to Richmond. Two reasons prompted this sudden decision: a natural concern for a man who in spite of his bitter hostility was still the only father he had ever known, and a hope that his son's presence might soften the old man's attitude, bringing back some of the affection he used to feel for him. This visit to a dying man was motivated by another, more practical reason for which Edgar could not be blamed. Mr. Allan had disinherited him, and it seemed certain that he was not mentioned in his father's will. If, somehow, there could be a reconciliation, perhaps Mr. Allan might change his will and leave Edgar a sum of money.

In March, 1834, Edgar arrived at his old home in Richmond. As he rang the bell and stood waiting, all the anguish of the dead years flooded his mind. The familiar house stirred up memories of Mrs. Frances Allan, the foster-mother he had loved, and of how she had cherished and protected him from his father's anger. Now he was to enter a home where he would find a second Mrs. Allan—one he had never seen before.

He heard the sound of footsteps and then the door was opened. An attractive woman in her mid-thirties stood in the doorway. She gazed at him, her eyes coldly formal. "Yes?" she questioned.

His glance was momentary, and then it passed beyond her into the house. Strange, clashing images made a confusion in his mind: the happy days of his childhood were mingled with the bitter scenes of failure and rejection that came with the later years.

"I've come to see Mr. Allan," he said abruptly.

"He can see no one," she answered. "He is seriously ill. His physicians have forbidden him to receive visitors." Her look had a touch of curiosity. She wondered who this odd-appearing young man could be. He acted as though he had not even heard her reply.

"I must see him," he said impatiently. Without warning he pushed her aside and entered the house, walking rapidly toward the stairway.

"Stop!" she cried. "You can't go up there."

Edgar hurried up the stairs and turned up the hallway toward the room that he remembered so well. The door was open, and he stood there, gazing at the old man who sat facing him, his cane propped against the side of his chair. Edgar felt a deep sense of pity as he noticed his father's thin face with its lines of suffering, and glimpsed the terrible swelling of his leg.

"Father!" he exclaimed. He took a step forward, his hands outstretched.

Mr. Allan started in surprise and his eyes scanned the son he had never expected to see again. There was no touch of tenderness or warmth in his glance. Instead, his face reddened and his eyes blazed with anger.

"Why are you here?" he shouted. "I don't want to see you. Get out!" He twisted wildly in his chair and grasped for his cane, raising it high above his head and shaking it violently. "Don't come near me!" he cried. "If you do—" His arm dropped and he slumped exhausted in his chair.

Behind Edgar Mrs. Allan's voice ordered, "Leave at once! Can't you see that you're making him ill? He doesn't want you here."

In a daze Edgar turned about and stumbled down the stairs. He had no recollection of how he had left the house until he found himself walking down the street, the cool air blowing against his fevered skin. Gripped by the agony of hopelessness, he made the return trip to Baltimore, back to the consoling sympathy of his Aunt Maria and his dear cousin Virginia. Of one thing Edgar was now certain: he would never see John Allan again.

Weeks later the expected news was received: Allan had died on March 27th, and two days later was buried in Shockoe Cemetery. In his will, lifetime provisions were made for Ann Moore Valentine, Edgar's Aunt Nancy, and for his wife, children and relatives—but not a cent was left to Edgar. He chose to ignore the young boy whom he had taken into his home with the understanding that he would provide for his future. But perhaps the most tragic failure of Allan's life had been his blindness—his inability to recognize the divine genius of the boy he had condemned and rejected. He had lived and died without understanding this, and without realizing that in his hands he had possessed the power to lessen the suffering of one who had been born with a magic gift of creativity.

In the small home on Amity Street the struggles of the Clemms and Edgar continued as before, except for one change. Young Henry Clemm, Aunt Maria's son, had left to try his fortune elsewhere. The passing weeks of close association strengthened an emotion within Edgar which he had tried to resist. For some months he had been aware of a deep affection for his little cousin, Virginia. She was a beautiful girl, delicate and fragile, with a pure white skin, large eyes with long lashes, and glossy black hair. Being together continuously, the natural fondness they shared as cousins was bound to develop into something stronger. It was true that Virginia was only twelve years old. But marriages were planned at an early age in the South; it was not at all uncommon, in those days, for a girl to be married at the age of thirteen or fourteen.

In succeeding months Edgar was to suffer an internal conflict. His love for Virginia and his hope of a future marriage could not conceal the obstacles—the fact that she was his cousin and that she was extremely young. Edgar was aware also that his relatives in Baltimore had strong sentiments against a marriage between Virginia and him. This was especially true of his cousin, Neilson Poe, who had offered to take Virginia into his home, where he and his wife would be responsible for her rearing and where she would be given a good education.

The year 1834, which had been launched promisingly, produced little except the distinction of having won the *Visiter's* contest. Through the assistance of his friend, John Pendleton Kennedy, one of his tales had been sold to the *Atlantic Souvenir,* an annual publication, for the small sum of fifteen dollars. But with this money spent, Edgar's situation was now so desperate that, on March 15, 1835, he wrote to Kennedy asking for his aid in obtaining a position as a school teacher.

Kennedy sent a cordial reply, inviting Edgar to come to his home for dinner. The receipt of the letter reduced Edgar to the lowest level of depression. As much as he wanted to, he could not accept Kennedy's invitation, for the simple reason that he had no decent clothes to wear. In despair, he decided to write the truth to Kennedy:

Dr. Sir,—Your kind invitation to dinner today has wounded me to the quick. I cannot come—and for reasons of the most humiliating nature in my personal appearance. You may conceive my deep mortification in making this disclosure to you—but it was necessary. If you will be my friend so far as to loan me $20, I will call on you tomorrow—otherwise it will be impossible, and I must submit to my fate.

Sincerely yours,

E. A. Poe

Kennedy was appalled upon receiving this letter. He had never dreamed that Edgar's situation was this bad. He proceeded to do everything he could for him, sending Edgar clothes, inviting him to dine regularly at the Kennedy home, and even offering him the use of a horse for exercise. But once started in aiding his fellow-man, Kennedy was not the type to stop with these measures. He knew that Edgar's most pressing need was for money, and that this could be realized best through the sale of his stories. Accordingly, he recommended Edgar's writing talents to the editor of the *Southern Literary Messenger,* advising Edgar to send one of his stories to the publication. Edgar submitted one of his strangest horror tales, *Berenice;* it was accepted and appeared in the *Messenger* in March, 1835. In the story of *Berenice,* Edgar showed himself once more to be fascinated by the atmosphere of death and by warped, ghastly impulses associated with it. The death of a beautiful woman, his favorite theme, occurs in a weird setting and is accompanied by horrifying actions.

As the story begins, Edgar paints his setting of brooding tragedy and of a man who lives in a world of strange distortion: "My baptismal name is Egaeus, that of my family I will not mention. Yet there are no towers in the land more time-honoured than my gloomy, grey, hereditary halls. . . ."

Egaeus is convinced that he has lived before—that his soul has had previous existence. In his present life, the realities of the world affect him as visions, "and as visions only, while the wild ideas of the land of dreams became, in turn, not the material of my every-day existence, but in very deed that existence utterly and solely itself."

Edgar set the stage for what was to happen later by creating a man with a disease of a "monomaniac character," one who would muse for hours over small, frivolous things, who might "become absorbed . . . in a quaint shadow . . ." or lose himself, "for an entire night, in watching the steady flame of a lamp . . . dream away whole days over the perfume of a flower . . . repeat, monotonously, some common word, until the sound, by dint of frequent repetition, ceased to convey any idea whatever to the mind. . . ." His monomania was a "morbid irritability of those properties of the mind in metaphysical science termed the *attentive.*"

For his lovely cousin Berenice, Egaeus' feelings *"had never been* of the heart . . . they *always were* of the mind." From an agile, graceful thing of beauty, Berenice is changed into an emaciated, dying woman; she is a victim of epilepsy, "a species . . . not infrequently terminating in *trance* itself—trance very nearly resembling positive dissolution, and from which her manner of recovery was, in most instances, startingly abrupt."

With the creation of the two characters, each afflicted with a strange illness, the tale moves to its fearful climax. Egaeus' "burning glances" fall upon Berenice's face. He studies her and tells of his sensations:

> The eyes were lifeless, and lustreless, and seemingly pupilless, and I shrank involuntarily from their glassy stare to the contemplation of the thin and shrunken lips. They parted; and in a smile of peculiar meaning, *the teeth* of the changed Berenice disclosed themselves slowly to my view. Would to God I had never beheld them, or that, having done so, I had died!

He is in the "full fury" of his monomania now. "The teeth!—the teeth!—they were here, and there, and everywhere, and visibly and palpably before me; long, narrow, and excessively white, with the pale lips writhing about them, as in the very moment of their terrible development."

His monomania will allow him no escape, and he is being driven toward a frightful act. Berenice is seized by epilepsy and soon a servant comes to tell him she is dead. ". . . the grave was ready for its tenant, and all the preparations for the burial were completed." The terrible deed he does in secret he cannot or will not recall. It has to do with a little box that lies on the table near him.

He hears of a "violated grave—of a disfigured body enshrouded, yet still breathing—still palpitating—*still alive!*" He discovers that his garments are "muddy and clotted with gore." When he shrieks and attempts to open the little box, it falls and bursts open.

". . . and from it, with a rattling sound, there rolled out some instruments of dental surgery, intermingled with thirty-two small, white, and ivory-looking substances that were scattered to and fro about the floor."

For Edgar, success was still slow in coming, but with the aid of Kennedy, he now began writing regularly for the *Southern Literary Messenger,* receiving small payments for articles and short stories. By mid-summer eleven of his stories had been published. The Richmond publisher of the *Messenger,* Thomas Willis White, quickly realized that in Edgar he had found a writer of unusual ability. In May, 1835, White wrote to ask Edgar if he would be willing to come to Richmond and take a steady position on the *Messenger.* Edgar's reply was ". . . nothing would give me greater pleasure."

Meanwhile, an expected tragedy was about to occur at home. Edgar's grandmother, Mrs. David Poe, nearing seventy-nine years, was on her deathbed. When she died on July 7th, the family's sadness was great. She had shared the poverty-stricken life and starvation with the others and had willingly contributed her small yearly pension of $240 to the household. Her death and the loss of her pension were both of serious consequence to the Clemm family. To Edgar, his grandmother's death was an occasion for sorrow and for a disturbing realization of his new responsibility. Somehow he must try to earn sufficient money to support his Aunt Maria and Virginia.

Following his unhappy experience at the University of Virginia, life had been a succession of hardships for Edgar. The boy who had swum six miles against the tide in the James River, and who was an excellent runner and boxer, was also an artist with a high-strung nervous system. In the past years he had been deeply wounded by a series of frustrations and failures, and had suffered intensely through the months of precarious living.

His trials included rejection by his foster-father, the death of his loved ones, the loss of his sweetheart Elmira, forced acceptance of a military life he hated, the misery of poverty and starvation, and disappointments in his creative work. These accumulated hardships had taken their toll of his health. Although he was only twenty-six years old, Edgar, in poor physical condition, had little resistance to illness and was often on the verge of collapse. His heart had never been strong, and there is some evidence that it may have been affected by the constant strain. In addition, the past had made him a person of a gloomy, despairing nature; he drifted into long periods of depression, and these, in turn, were bound to weaken him physically and nervously.

He refers to one of these periods of illness on May 30th, when he writes to Thomas White, "I have not seen Mr. Kennedy for some days, having been too unwell to go abroad . . ." Two weeks later he writes, "I am glad to say that I have entirely recovered—although Dr. Buckler, no longer than three weeks ago, assured me that nothing but a sea-voyage would save me . . ."

The frequency of his illnesses and his tendency toward withdrawal have led to speculations about the regularity of his drinking—and even his possible use of drugs. Had Edgar taken to using the easily obtainable drugs of that day—morphine or salt of opium, laudanum or wine of opium? The strange dream world of a number of his *Tales of the Folio Club,* the fantasies of the mind, the weird images, the odd language—these seem to indicate that he wrote of what he glimpsed and felt in an opiate reverie. The distorted scenes in his stories *Berenice* and *Ligeia* may offer evidence of this.

In April, 1842, in a story published in *Graham's Magazine* titled *Life in Death,* Edgar, through the main character, describes experiences with opium:

At length I bethought me of a little packet of opium which lay with my tobacco in my hookah case, for at Constantinople I had acquired the habit of smoking the weed with the drug. I sought and found the narcotic. But when about to cut off a portion I felt the necessity of hesitation. In smoking it was a matter of little importance how much was employed. Usually I half-filled the bowl of the hookah with opium and tobacco cut and mingled, half and half. Sometimes when I had used the whole of this mixture I experienced no very peculiar effects; at other times I would not have smoked the pipe more than two-thirds out, when symptoms of mental derangement, which were even alarming, warned me to desist. But the effect proceeded with an easy gradation which deprived the indulgence of all danger. Here, however, the case was different. I had never swallowed opium before. . . .

In later versions of the story, its title changed to *The Oval Portrait,* the long passage containing details of opium use was omitted.

Other references to the effects of opium are found in *The Fall of the House of Usher,* where Roderick Usher speaks in the manner of "the irreclaimable eater of opium, during the periods of his most intense excitement." In *Ligeia,* the death of the exquisite Ligeia leads her lover to turn to "such follies, even in childhood," for which he had "imbibed a taste." He bemoans, "I had become a bounden slave in the trammels of opium, and my labors and my orders had taken a coloring from my dreams."

A consideration of Edgar's astonishing output of poems, stories, and articles has raised the question of how he managed to do all this in his general state of low energy and poor health. The theory has been advanced that his creative drive was stimulated artificially through the use of opium. Charles Baudelaire, the French poet and critic, who in his short life indulged to excess in liquor and opium, expressed the belief that the strange visions and fantasies that Edgar created in his stories were experienced in opium dreams.

On the other hand, Dr. Thomas Dunn English, a Philadelphia physician who had known Edgar as early as 1839 and had spent some time with him, denied emphatically that Edgar had ever been an opium user. In the *Independent* of October 15, 1896, English stated,

Had Poe the opium habit when I knew him, I should both as a physician and a man of observation, have discovered it during his frequent visits to my rooms, my visits at his house, and our meetings elsewhere— I saw no signs of it and believe the charge to be a baseless slander.

Whether Edgar used opium regularly, or whether his fearful world of phantasms, decay, and madness was simply the invention of a genius whose imagination soared into regions where none had gone before, has never been settled.

In the late summer of 1835 he said goodbye to Baltimore and a temporary farewell to Aunt Maria and Virginia. He was returning to Richmond, a city of painful memories, to aid Thomas White on the *Southern Literary Messenger*. His aunt and Virginia were to join him as soon as possible. Now, each change would lead him upward to the height of his career. He was to demonstrate an astonishing versatility, writing, with equal ease, in the fields of poetry, the short story, and literary criticism.

8 · *Marriage, Literary Criticism, and the Scientific Mind*

UPON returning to Richmond, undoubtedly in an optimistic state, Edgar first visited the Mackenzies, where his sister, Rosalie, and his friend, Jack, were happy to see him. Rosalie, now twenty-four years old, was a sweet, lovable girl who adored her brother "Eddy." But it had been evident from her early years that her mental development would be quite limited; she was destined to be a simple girl, capable of adapting to life and managing her own affairs but completely lacking in the intellectual development displayed by her brother.

Edgar reported for work at the offices of the *Messenger* at the corner of Main and Fifteenth Streets. There he was greeted by Thomas White, who made it plain that Edgar was to do much of the editorial work while White concentrated upon increasing the newspaper's circulation—at present a mere 700. In spite of the small salary at which he was starting, Edgar had good reasons for being grateful to White. Following the appearance in print of *Berenice* in March, 1835, the *Messenger* had opened its columns to other stories by Edgar. *Morella* was published in April, *Lionizing* in May, and in June there appeared a tale that Edgar had first imagined in his early Richmond days when he gazed at the heavens through his small telescope. Delighted *Messenger* subscribers read the story of *Hans Pfaall* and his *Voyage to the Moon,* chuckling over the antics of the impudent Hans and over Edgar's spoof of space travel, while at the same time marveling over the learned display of scientific data and reasoning.

Edgar took up lodgings at the boarding house of Mrs. Poore, in Capitol Square. He resumed many old Richmond friendships, but in spite of this he soon became quite lonely. He missed his Aunt Maria, and especially the young girl he had come to love dearly—his little cousin, Virginia.

Nevertheless, a return to surroundings of the past was bound to bring him in contact with his first young love, Elmira, now Mrs. A. Barrett Shelton. At an elaborate party given in a large mansion, Edgar, somehow aware that she would be there, stationed himself in a window nook that commanded a view of the upstairs drawing room. Later she walked up the stairs alone, and, as though she felt the intense power of his gaze, turned to discover him. Their glances remained fixed, and the two stood motionless. Both were too overcome to speak a word. Behind Elmira her husband suddenly appeared; the situation was instantly apparent to his jealous eyes. He and Elmira did not stay for the remainder of the party. She was bundled into her cloak and rushed out of the house by her angry husband.

In August, Edgar received a letter from his aunt which threw him into a state bordering on panic. Already lonely and depressed, he was shocked by his aunt's mention of the Neilson Poes and her hints at possible changes in Virginia's future. She had brought up the question of Neilson's willingness to take Virginia into his luxurious home and make provisions for her support and education. Edgar had known for some time that his cousin Neilson was strongly opposed to Virginia's staying in the Clemm household and to any thought of an engagement or marriage between her and Edgar.

On August 29th, Edgar wrote a long letter to his aunt. It was filled with uncontrolled anguish and sorrow. To his "dearest Aunty" he composed a self-pitying appeal, saying, "I am blinded with tears while writing this letter—I have no wish to live another hour."

The letter continues in a suffering and pleading tone: "I love, *you know* I love Virginia passionately devotedly. I cannot express in words the fervent devotion I feel towards my dear little cousin —my own darling. But what can I say. Oh think for me for I am incapable of thinking. All my thoughts are occupied with the supposition that both you & she will prefer to go with N. Poe; I do sincerely believe that your *comforts* will for the present be secured— I cannot speak as regards your peace—your happiness. You both have tender hearts—and you will always have the reflection that my agony is more than I can bear—that you have driven me to the grave—for love like mine can never be gotten over. It is useless to disguise the truth that when Virginia goes with N. P. that I shall never behold her again—that is absolutely sure."

In admitting that he is incapable of giving advice to his aunt, Edgar asks, "Can I, in honor & in truth say Virginia! do not go!—do not go where you can be comfortable & perhaps happy— and on the other hand can I calmly resign my—life itself. If she had truly loved me would she not have rejected the offer with scorn? Oh God have mercy on me! . . ."

Edgar then explains that he has rented a "sweet little house" on Church Hill for only five dollars a month. He had dreamed of living there with his aunt and his wife, but now he says, ". . . the dream is over God have mercy on me. What have I to *live for?* Among strangers with not one soul to love me."

He writes that Thomas White has promised to pay him a salary of $60 a month and that "we could live in comparative comfort & happiness—even the $4 a week I am now paying for board would support us all—but I shall have $15 a week & what need would we have of more?"

Later, in referring to his aunt's words, he says, "You speak of Virginia acquiring accomplishments, and entering into society— you speak in so *worldly* a tone. Are you sure she would be more happy— Do you think any one could love her more dearly than I? She will have far—very far better opportunity of entering into society here than with N. P. Every one here receives me with open arms."

He closes asking his aunt to "Kiss her for me—a million times." In a special postscript to Virginia he writes, "My love, my own sweetest Sissy, my darling little wifey, think well before you break the heart of your cousin Eddy." From the irregular, almost illegible scrawl, the wavering lines and blots, it was evident that he was in a condition of extreme mental and physical disturbance. That he may have been drinking during this time of distress is entirely probable. Past events indicate that he turned to liquor when his problems overwhelmed him.

To Edgar, continued work on the *Messenger* was not possible until this personal matter was settled. In September he returned suddenly to Baltimore, and the records show that he took out a license to marry Virginia. But the marriage did not occur at this time. He wrote to Thomas White from Baltimore, and White's answering letter reveals that Edgar had been drinking to excess, that it had affected his work on the newspaper, and that Edgar now promised to turn over a new leaf. White's answer was sympathetic and encouraging:

That you are sincere in all your promises, I firmly believe. But Edgar, when you once again tread these streets, I have my fears that your resolve would fall again,—and that you would again sip the juice, even till it stole away your senses. Rely on your own strength and you are gone! Look to your Maker for help, and you are safe!

White's fatherly advice continues in a practical vein:

If you could make yourself contented to take up your quarters in my family, or in any other private family where liquor is not used, I should think there was hopes of you.—But, if you go to a tavern, or to any other place where it is used at table, you are not safe. I speak from experience.

In praising Edgar for his "fine talents," White pointed out that one who wants others to respect him and his talents, *must learn to respect himself*. "Separate yourself from the bottle, and from bottle companions, for ever!" White urged.

He insists strongly,

If you should come to Richmond again, and again should be an assistant in my office, it must be especially understood by us that all engagements on my part would be dissolved, the moment you get drunk.

No man is safe who drinks before breakfast! No man can do so, and attend to business properly.

Edgar's loneliness and his shock at the prospect of losing Virginia had caused him to drink. That he could change when his problems were solved was demonstrated in his behavior of the following months. In October, 1835, he brought his aunt and Virginia with him to Richmond, and by the middle of the month he had returned to work on the *Messenger*. The three took rooms at Mrs. James Yarrington's boarding house near Capitol Square.

Now the short stories, articles of criticism, and literary notices fairly streamed from his prolific pen. The *Messenger* featured his new stories, *Shadow—A Fable, King Pest the First,* and an older one, *Loss of Breath*. But in the succeeding year, his frank, individualistic reviews of books, mainly by American authors, helped establish his reputation as an outspoken literary critic. His natural independence of thought would not allow him to follow the examples of other reviewers who wrote "puffs" of books, praising them exaggeratedly and beyond all reason. His tremendous background in reading had taught him not only how to criticize a literary work, but also how to detect mediocre writing. He persisted in writing his blunt, constructive opinions, having confidence in his own judgment and refusing to permit anything dishonest to creep into his reviews. Above all, as a writer who valued originality and bold, new ideas, he was not one to accept conventional standards blindly. When, in his personal opinion, a book was of high quality, even though it did not follow accepted standards, he praised it without restraint.

While much could be said of the "credit side" for his frank evaluations, he was also guilty of a type of criticism which can be placed only on the "debit side." On occasion he lowered himself to write bitter, sneering criticism of books, to launch personal attacks against authors, and to make insulting remarks about them in the *Messenger*. It seemed, at times, as though he were releasing some of his frustration and the anger against the world that burned inside him. At other times, he appeared to pour out his scathing language merely to stir up controversy and attract attention.

Because of his bold criticisms, the series of articles in the *Messenger* placed him in the literary limelight and brought him both friends and bitter enemies. But to the *Messenger* it brought something quite gratifying: an increase of subscriptions from the original 700 to more than 3,500.

To illustrate the volume and variety of writings that were produced by his fertile mind, an estimate of works published in the *Messenger* in 1835 includes the following: thirty-seven book and periodical reviews, nine stories, four poems, and portions of his drama *Politian*. In 1836, for the *Messenger* Edgar is credited with more than eighty reviews, six poems, four essays, and three stories.

His drama in blank verse, *Politian,* which he never finished, appeared in sections in the *Messenger;* three scenes were printed in December, 1835, and two more in January, 1836. Edgar's interest had been aroused by a real life "Kentucky Tragedy" which had caused a sensation when it occurred in Frankfort, Kentucky in 1825. Solomon P. Sharp, a distinguished lawyer, had seduced Anne Cooke. Later, when Jereboam Beauchamp fell in love with her and proposed marriage, she at first refused. After much persuasion by Beauchamp, she told him the story of her betrayal, and the conditions under which she would marry him: "Before we are married you must promise me to kill Sharp!"

A challenge to a duel was ignored by Sharp. Anne Cooke married Beauchamp but could not forget what had happened, and finally threatened to kill Sharp herself. Unable to restrain himself, Beauchamp went to Sharp's home and stabbed him to death. He was tried and sentenced to be hanged. His wife chose to join him in his cell, and later, by agreement, they both attempted suicide. She died, but Beauchamp lived to be executed on July 7, 1826. During their imprisonment she had written *Poetical Pieces* and he had produced his *Confession*. When these were published they created a furor, and a number of American authors used the exciting, melodramatic incidents for stage dramas and novels.

In creating his tragic drama *Politian,* Edgar changed the setting to Rome, with his main character becoming an Englishman. Politian, the Earl of Leicester, falls in love with Lalage without seeing her, enchanted by the sound of her voice as she sings a melancholy song. In the impetuous nobleman was Edgar really drawing a portrait of himself? In the play Alessandro inquires, "I have heard much of this Politian. Gay, volatile and giddy—is he not, and little given to thinking?"

In the discussion that follows, it appears that Politian is a man of much achievement and many moods. There is "no branch . . . of all philosophy so deep abstruse he has not mastered it. Learned as few are learned." But he is also seen as "one who entered madly into life, drinking the cup of pleasure to the dregs." By others

Politian is called "a dreamer, and a man shut out from common passions"; and a speaker finally asks, "Did I dream, or did I hear Politian was a *melancholy* man?"

The writer who could turn from his world of fantasy and the supernatural to the cold, precise world of the review and essay had still more versatility to demonstrate. One side of Edgar's mind appraised events deliberately and logically. He was adept in applying scientific deduction, and, if necessary, could draw upon his strong background in mathematics.

Some years earlier, Edgar had become intrigued over the performances of a strange mechanical figure, called an automaton or android, then on exhibition in the United States. The details of the automaton's history were in themselves sufficient to fascinate him. It was a mechanical Chess-Player, and since its invention by the Baron Wolfgang von Kempelen in 1769, it had "toured" the continent, challenging any and all opponents to play against it. Some illustrious personages who had played games with the automaton included the Empress Maria Theresa of Austria, Frederick the Great of Prussia, Louis XVIII of France, George III of England, and Napoleon I. While in France, in 1783, Benjamin Franklin was invited to play the automatic chess-wizard. He agreed and was soundly beaten.

Baron von Kempelen died in 1804 and the Chess-Player was sold to J. N. Maelzel, the clever inventor of the metronome. Soon he placed the automaton on exhibition in America, demonstrating its skill at a theater in Baltimore. Maelzel's Chess-Player became a sensation; the baffled observers were unable to figure out how it managed to beat all its opponents. In March, 1836, the Chess-Player arrived in Richmond. Edgar did not attend its performance, but received details of its appearance from his friends.

One day Edgar sat considering an idea that had been in his mind for some time. A challenge to his deductive powers—his unusual skill in piling up facts until he reached a conclusion that could not be disputed—always aroused his interest. He stared at the paper before him and grinned. It had not been necessary for him to watch the Chess-Player; he already had a definite theory about its operation.

He pictured the figure as his friends had described it. The Chess-Player, constructed as a giant Turk, with its head wrapped in a brilliantly colored turban, sat cross-legged behind a low wooden chest. The mechanical man clutched a long-stemmed pipe in his left hand and amused the audience by moving his head and rolling his eyes. He seemed to pause and think before he made a play. A nod of his head indicated that he had given a check to the king. The audience had been astonished by the demonstration that the Chess-Player could not be fooled. A false move brought a quick response: the Chess-Player rapped on the chest with his right hand, shook his head vigorously, and moved the piece back to its former position. Astonishingly, he could even speak one word—the word "echec," which he sounded in a deep muffled tone whenever his opponent was checkmated.

Edgar had already noted a significant point which gave him a partial explanation of the automaton's operation. Maelzel's Chess-Player held the pipe for only a short time before the game began. Once play started, the pipe was removed and the automaton made all the moves with his left hand. Edgar nodded and began to write. The Chess-Player had baffled both mechanics and scientists, and he could not refrain from showing his amazement at their theories and scoffing at them in his opening statement:

Perhaps no exhibition of the kind has ever elicited so general attention as the Chess-Player of Maelzel. Wherever seen it has been an object of intense curiosity to all persons who think. Yet the question of its *modus operandi* is still undetermined . . . we find everywhere men of mechanical genius, of great general acuteness and discriminative understanding, who make no scruple in pronouncing the Automaton a *pure machine,* unconnected with human agency in its movements, and consequently, beyond all comparison, the most astonishing of the inventions of mankind.

Edgar smiled and went on to add, "And such it would undoubtedly be, were they right in their supposition." As he wrote he thought of other mechanical devices that were capable of amazing performances. Since 1822, Charles Babbage, the famous English mathematician, had been discussing plans for a calculating machine. Edgar pointed out that the very concept of a machine that could compute perfectly and then print the results was sufficient to stagger the imagination. But Mr. Babbage's calculating machine is beneath comparison with as complicated a creation as the Chess-Player—*if the Player is a pure machine,* "and performs its operations without any immediate human agency."

But is the Chess-Player a *pure machine,* Edgar asked? In a calculating machine, one step follows upon another; once the data are given, the machine must move in a "succession of unerring steps liable to no change." Anyone, Edgar explained, can understand the possibility of arranging a mechanism of this type, that moves toward a solution without deviating. "But the case is widely different with the Chess-Player." The moves in a game of chess cannot be anticipated. No step is certain, since different players would advise different moves. To Edgar, a machine whose movements would be "necessarily interrupted and disarranged" by the opposing moves of a human chess-player, and that would still be flexible enough to readjust, change its plans, and meet the new situation, would be, "beyond all comparison, the most wonderful of the inventions of mankind!" Obviously, no such machine could be constructed.

Based upon what he had learned about the Chess-Player's appearance, and the details of the box-like apparatus that served as a table for the immovable chess-board, Edgar proceeded to offer a logical analysis, as superbly planned as a surgeon's operation or a scientist's dissection. He was now both the scientist and the detective—solving the mystery with the same brilliant deduction he would use in *The Gold Bug,* in the cryptograms that he delighted in decoding, and in his creation of the detective story with its analytical genius, Monsieur C. Auguste Dupin.

First, Edgar felt, certain details concerning the exhibition and the actions of Maelzel, the exhibitor, should be examined:

At the hour appointed for exhibition, a curtain is withdrawn, or folding doors are thrown open, and the machine rolled to within about twelve feet of the nearest of the spectators, between whom and it (the machine) a rope is stretched. The exhibitor will, if requested, roll the machine to any portion of the room, suffer it to remain altogether on any designated spot, or even shift its location repeatedly during the progress of a game. The bottom of the box is elevated considerably above the floor by means of the castors or brazen rollers on which it moves, a clear view of the surface immediately beneath the Automaton being thus afforded to the spectators. The chair on which the figure sits is affixed permanently to the box.

Painstakingly, Edgar described the construction of the mechanical man, and gave all the remaining details of its operation. Maelzel appeared disarmingly frank, opening the doors of the long chest to display a mass of machinery to the spectators, and even opening a rear door while holding a lighted candle to demonstrate that nothing was concealed, and that the machinery supposedly occupied the entire interior. The chest had three large compartments covered by folding doors, but at the close of Maelzel's demonstration the spectators were convinced that they had seen the contents of all three. Maelzel even turned the automaton entirely around to allow the audience to inspect the back.

As the chess-match begins, Maelzel winds up the machine and the Chess-Player takes the first move, playing with his left hand. The match is usually limited to a half-hour, and the Chess-Player almost always wins; he has been beaten only once or twice.

Edgar considered solutions that had been offered. The theory that Maelzel operated the huge Turk by mechanical means, he discarded at once. This was not possible, since the machine was rolled about on castors. The theory that magnets were used was also illogical. Maelzel encouraged spectators to bring as many magnets as they liked, to demonstrate that there was nothing in the apparatus that could be pulled into place by outside magnets.

In presenting his own theory, Edgar stressed what he believed to be the deciding points. The fact that the Turk did not make his moves at regular intervals, "goes to prove that regularity is unimportant to the action of the Automaton—in other words, that the Automaton is not *a pure machine.*" Summing up this and other evidence, Edgar concluded that the Chess-Player's moves are *not* regulated by Maelzel, whose back is turned toward an opponent who may change his mind and withdraw his chess piece, at which time the Automaton also "changes" its mind, stops it motion, and chooses a different move. Since Maelzel is not watching the player, it appears obvious that he is not manipulating the machine, but, as Edgar explained, "that its movements are regulated by *mind—* by some person who sees the board of the antagonist."

Edgar's scientific inductive method led to one solution: the person who sees the board at all times and who directs the Chess-Player's movements with *his mind,* is obviously concealed in the large chest. He is, of course, a master chess-player. When Maelzel displays the opened compartments, one at a time, the man shifts his position so as to remain concealed. Who could this man be? To this Edgar offered a triumphant explanation:

There is a man, *Schlumberger,* who attends him (Maelzel) wherever he goes, but who has no ostensible occupation other than that of assisting in the packing and unpacking of the Automaton. This man is about medium size, and has a remarkable stoop in the shoulders. Whether he professes to play chess or not, we are not informed. It is quite certain, however, that he is never to be seen during the exhibition of the Chess-Player, although frequently visible just before and just after the exhibition.

Some time ago, Edgar recalled for the reader, Maelzel visited Richmond with his Chess-Player. On that occasion, when Schlumberger was suddenly taken ill, there was no exhibition. "These facts are well known to many of our citizens," said Edgar. "The reason assigned for the suspension of the Chess-Player's performances was *not* the illness of *Schlumberger. The inferences from all this we leave, without farther comment, to the reader."*

In a final flourish of his brilliant logic, Edgar could not resist one amazing bit of deduction. Why did the Chess-Player always use his left arm? "A circumstance so remarkable cannot be accidental," said Edgar. He was the only one to notice it and realize its significance. The use of the left arm had to do with the position of the man concealed in the interior:

"The Automaton plays with his left arm, because under no other circumstances could the man within play with his right—a *desideratum* of course." The man hidden in the box would find himself in an "exceedingly painful and awkward position" and would be unable to manipulate the Automaton's moves for any length of time, *if the Chess-Player were to use the right arm.* As he crouched there, the man (presumably Schlumberger) was able to bring his right arm across his chest, and his right fingers could easily move the machinery in the shoulder of the Automaton. In concluding this astonishingly detailed analysis, Edgar stated modestly, "We do not believe that any reasonable objections can be urged against this solution of the Automaton Chess-Player"!

Between the strenuous periods of writing, Edgar found time to make his most important decision, and to persuade his aunt and Virginia to agree. On May 16, 1836, a marriage bond was signed in the Hustings Court of Richmond between Virginia and Edgar. In an oath that was made before the clerk of the court, and witnessed by Thomas W. Cleland, a friend of Edgar's, the young bride-to-be was described as "of the full age of twenty-one years." Actually, Virginia E. Clemm had not yet reached fourteen. That evening the Reverend Amasa Converse, a Presbyterian minister, performed the ceremony at Mrs. Yarrington's boarding house, and later the newlyweds departed for a honeymoon at Petersburg, Virginia.

For Edgar, his little cousin Virginia, shaped with childlike delicacy and possessing an ivory skin, glowing eyes, and a high forehead, was the ideal woman. In the years they had lived with his aunt he had grown to love her deeply; to him she represented the fulfillment of his dream of ideal beauty which in his earlier years had appeared in his poem, *To Helen*. Something in his frail, almost ethereal wife became attuned to the sadness and melancholy that were part of his nature, so that he saw her at times in a tragic setting, centered in the sorrow and suffering that seemed inevitable in life.

In his story *Berenice,* she had at first been "agile, graceful, and overflowing with energy." Later, "Disease—a fatal disease, fell like the simoon upon her frame." But no matter what his imagination added, Berenice's features resembled Virginia's: "The forehead was high, and very pale, and singularly placid . . ."

In the future, when he was to write his story *Eleonora,* she would come to life in his thoughts of Virginia:

She whom I loved in youth, and of whom I now pen calmly and distinctly these remembrances, was the sole daughter of the only sister of my mother long departed. Eleonora was the name of my cousin. We had always dwelled together, beneath a tropical sun, in the Valley of the Many-Colored Grass.

He painted the picture of their private world, "the Valley of the Many-Colored Grass," as he preferred it: "Thus it was that we lived all alone, knowing nothing of the world without the valley—I, and my cousin, and her mother."

Again, in the story, *Ligeia,* the features of the tall, "somewhat slender" lady Ligeia were, in part, a re-creation of his beloved Virginia:

I examined the contour of the lofty and pale forehead—it was faultless—how cold indeed that word when applied to a majesty so divine!—the skin rivalling the purest ivory, the commanding extent and repose, the gentle prominence of the regions above the temples; and then the raven-black, the glossy, the luxuriant, and naturally-curling tresses. . . .

While most of his waking hours were spent in writing and editing, Edgar, as a married man, devoted some effort in an attempt to make practical plans for the future. A proposition suggested by Thomas White that Edgar and his family share a new home with the Whites did not work out. The house had been purchased by White for $10,000, and his offer was to rent it to Edgar's aunt who was to take charge and board White's family. After contracting for more than $200 worth of furniture on credit, Edgar discovered that the house was too small for two families. In this dilemma, on June 7, 1836, he wrote to his friend, John Pendleton Kennedy: "Having got into a little temporary difficulty I venture to ask you, once more, for aid, rather than apply to any of my new friends in Richmond."

Meanwhile, Edgar discovered that his brilliant work on the *Messenger,* which caused much comment in literary circles, had made little impression upon the important publishers. His greatest hope was that a volume of his short stories would be printed. Turned down by Carey and Lea, he obtained the help of James K. Paulding, who persuaded Harper & Brothers to read his works. To Edgar's bitter disappointment, they rejected his stories, offering criticisms which seemed to indicate that the stories were not in the public taste. They objected to the fact that most of them had already appeared in print, but also commented that "they consisted of detached tales and pieces; . . . Readers in this country have a decided and strong preference for works (especially fiction) in which a single and connected story occupies the whole volume. . . ." Thus, the new short story form, which Edgar had developed, was rejected without a second thought!

A further objection was that "The papers are too learned and mystical. They would be understood and relished only by a very few—not by the multitude." In conclusion, Harper & Brothers believed that it was for Edgar's own interest not to publish the stories, since, as a new author, he would be unable to "overcome the injurious effect of a first failure."

While he was at first eager to work on the *Messenger* and grateful for the opportunity White had granted him, Edgar found that the increasing conflict between White and himself made his situation extremely difficult. Edgar assumed that he was Editor of the *Messenger,* and White referred to him as "Editor" in official correspondence, but in practice White controlled the newspaper with a firm hand and a critical eye, seeming reluctant to give Edgar complete authority. For some of this reluctance he cannot be blamed. There is evidence that the two men quarreled and that the cause, at times, was the familiar one: Edgar's periodic drinking, followed by days of illness and inaction.

In September, 1836, White notified Edgar that their association was ended. The two patched things up, but on December 27, 1836, in a letter to Nathaniel Beverley Tucker, a critic, author, and

Professor of Law, White made it plain that he was discharging Edgar:

Highly as I really think of Mr. Poe's talents, I shall be forced to give him notice in a week or so at farthest that I can no longer recognize him as editor of my *Messenger*. Three months ago I felt it my duty to give him a similar notice,—and was afterwards over-persuaded to restore him to his situation on certain conditions—which conditions he has again forfeited.

Obviously, the "certain conditions" refer to Edgar's promise not to drink—a promise which he did not keep. Four years later, Edgar wrote a letter explaining his side of the story, and offering other reasons for his decision to quit the *Messenger*:

The drudgery was excessive, the salary was contemptible. In fact, I soon found that whatever reputation I might personally gain, this reputation would be all. I stood no chance of bettering my pecuniary condition, while my best energies were wasted in the service of an illiterate and vulgar, although well meaning man, who had neither the capacity to appreciate my labors, nor the will to reward them.

Edgar's editorship of the *Messenger* ended some time in January, 1837, with several of his poems and reviews appearing in that issue of the newspaper. In the January *Messenger* there appeared the first installment of a story whose details had been stored in his remarkable mind ever since his boyhood voyage to England and his experiences with boats on the James River. *The Narrative of Arthur Gordon Pym,* with its blood-curdling details of "a Mutiny and Atrocious Butchery on board the American Brig Grampus," was the longest story Edgar had so far attempted. A second installment was printed in the *Messenger* in February, after its author had severed all connections with the paper.

That same month, with no guarantee of any future employment, Edgar, accompanied by his aunt and Virginia, set off for New York. There, within a short time, he achieved an important success. Harper & Brothers, who had encouraged him to write a long narrative, agreed to publish *The Narrative of Arthur Gordon Pym.* Edgar had made a promising beginning in the great metropolis, but his stay there would not be long; it was Philadelphia that beckoned him, and in the summer of 1838 he moved to that bustling, growing city. He had lived a life of terrible sacrifice, finding himself always blocked by an immovable barrier in his search for the elusive recognition. But now the barrier was to crumble before the out-pouring of his great talent. Fame was within his grasp.

9 · *Tales of Death and Terror*

Ligeia— Ligeia—" Edgar murmured the words as though in a dream, while he stared at the paper before him. The vision of the ideal beauty of a maiden named Ligeia had been with him ever since his early youth. In *Al Aaraaf* he had exclaimed,

> Ligeia! Ligeia!
>   My beautiful one!
> Whose harshest idea
>   Will to melody run,

And as the poem continued he wrote,

> Ligeia! wherever
>   Thy image may be,
> No magic shall sever
>   Thy music from thee.

But now his imagination drove him to write a story about the lady Ligeia. In appearance, she was bound to resemble his beloved Virginia, but otherwise, as he wrote, he created a woman of intellect, perhaps because he felt the lack of this quality in his young wife:

I have spoken of the learning of Ligeia: it was immense—such as I have never known in woman. In the classical tongues was she deeply proficient, and as far as my own acquaintance extended in regard to the modern dialects of Europe, I have never known her at fault.

As he tells the tale in the first person, inevitably, from his first words, he creates the atmosphere of tragedy—of the death of a beautiful woman.

He writes in the way he loves: he must live within the strange scenes he creates—it is *his* life with Ligeia:

I cannot for my soul, remember how, when or even precisely where, I first became acquainted with the lady Ligeia . . . a recollection flashes upon me that I have *never known* the paternal name of her who was my friend and my betrothed, and who became the partner of my studies, and finally the wife of my bosom.

Ligeia's face floats before him in an image so clear that he can trace the features. Her beauty is not of the "regular mould," he tells himself. The key is in the words of Francis Bacon: "There is no exquisite beauty without some *strangeness* in the proportion."

Always close to him, reaching out to grasp the ones he loved, were the skeleton fingers of death: "Ligeia grew ill. The wild eyes blazed with a too—too glorious effulgence; the pale fingers became of the transparent waxen hue of the grave. . . ." But Ligeia has a strong desire for life and a passionate rebellion against death. She recites her agony and protest to her lover, instructing him to repeat certain verses. Here, in the midst of the story, Edgar chose to turn to poetry to paint the terror of death, with its hero, "the conqueror worm":

> Lo! 'tis a gala night
>   Within the lonesome latter years
> An angel throng, bewinged, bedight
>   In veils, and drowned in tears,
> Sit in a theatre, to see
>   A play of hopes and fears,
> While the orchestra breathes fitfully
>   The music of the spheres.

Within "that motley drama" a crowd chases a Phantom for evermore and never seizes it, traveling "Through a circle that ever returneth in to the self-same spot." Then comes the terrifying end to life's futile drama, whose characters are "mimes" and "mere puppets":

> But see, amid the mimic rout
>   A crawling shape intrude!
> A blood-red thing that writhes from out
>   The scenic solitude!
> It writhes!—it writhes!—with mortal pangs
>   The mimes become its food,
> And the seraphs sob at vermin fangs
>   In human gore imbued.
>
> Out—out are the lights—out all!
>   And over each quivering form,

The curtain, a funeral pall,
Comes down with the rush of a storm—
And the angels, all pallid and wan,
Uprising, unveiling, affirm
That the play is the tragedy, "Man,"
And its hero, the conqueror Worm.

Ligeia now shrieks in protest against death, appealing to God for aid against the "conqueror worm," and crying, "shall this conqueror be not once conquered?" As she dies, her lover hears a low murmur from her lips: *"Man doth not yield him to the angels, nor unto death utterly, save only through the weakness of his feeble will."*

Ligeia has within her the determination and the strength to defeat the "conqueror worm"; there is no feebleness in her will. The story rises to a fearful climax, with the lady Ligeia returning from the grave to reappear before her lover, facing him in the enshrouded corpse of his second wife.

The story *Ligeia* with its ghastly "conqueror worm" was printed in a Baltimore periodical, the *American Museum,* in the fall of 1838. Meanwhile, Poe and his family had moved from temporary lodgings in Philadelphia to a small house on Sixteenth Street. Edgar resumed a friendship with James Pedder, an Englishman whom he had met in New York. Pedder, a writer and editor, did his best to obtain assignments for Edgar in Philadelphia publications.

To aid Edgar, who as usual was almost without funds, Pedder arranged for him to edit a book which certainly could not have provided him with any inspiration. A textbook, it was titled *The Conchologist's First Book,* and contained illustrations of 215 shells. Edgar hastily assembled the contents of the book, which was "arranged expressly for the use of schools," patterning it after similar popular texts. Later he was accused of plagiarism—of actually reprinting the major portion of a textbook by Captain Thomas Brown. In a letter to a friend, Edgar denied the charge, saying,

I wrote it in conjunction with Professor Thomas Wyatt, and Professor McMurtrie, of Philadelphia—my name being put to the work, as best known and most likely to aid its circulation. I wrote the Preface and Introduction, and translated from Cuvier, the accounts of the animals, etc. *All* School-books are necessarily made in a similar way. The very title-page acknowledges that the animals are given "according to Cuvier."

At home, Edgar found many happy moments in the hours he spent with Virginia and his aunt. In his spare time, he worked to improve his young wife's education. From his earliest days he had possessed a deep love for music, and had enjoyed singing and playing simple melodies on the flute. Because of this, and his affection for Virginia, he encouraged her to sing and to learn how to play accompaniments on the harp. Whenever company came to the house, Edgar was delighted if he could persuade his pretty wife to sing a few songs. To him, Virginia's modest performances provided a glowing pleasure that he seldom found elsewhere.

In spite of this pleasure, the problem of employment remained his constant worry. In April, 1839, Edgar wrote to William E. Burton, owner and editor of *Burton's Gentlemen's Magazine,* suggesting that the two pool their efforts, editing the magazine jointly. On May 11th, Burton replied with enthusiasm, saying:

I have given your proposal a fair consideration. I wish to form some such engagement as that which you have proposed, and know of no one more likely to suit my views than yourself.

In the remainder of the letter, Burton offered the details of the employment:

Shall we say ten dollars per week for the remaining portion of this year? Should we remain together, which I see no reason to negative, your proposition shall be in force for 1840. A month's notice to be given on either side previous to a separation.

Two hours a day, except occasionally, will, I believe, be sufficient for all required, except in the production of any article of you own. At all events you could easily find time for any other light avocation—supposing that you did not exercise your talents in behalf of any publication interfering with the prospects of the G.M.

Edgar was, of course, pleased and excited at this new opportunity. Above all, he was seeking a magazine that would print his stories and poems, and his position with the *Gentlemen's Magazine* would guarantee this. In the late summer of 1839, he completed work on a story whose theme of dread and decay was to make it one of the most powerful he had ever created. To reproduce the full flavor of gloom and terror, as always, Edgar found it necessary to place himself in the story—to make himself the observer watching the fearful events, seeing them head inevitably toward the tragic ending. He was a master in the creation of an ominous, brooding atmosphere and the morbid feelings that accompanied it. From the very first strokes of his gloomy pen, he leads the reader into the shadows where terror hides:

During the whole of a dull, dark, and resoundless day in the autumn of the year, when the clouds hung oppressively low in the heavens, I had been passing alone, on horseback, through a singularly dreary tract of country, and at length found myself, as the shades of evening drew on, within view of the melancholy House of Usher.

The House of Usher is painted as a "mansion of gloom," with "bleak walls" and "vacant eye-like windows." As he lives through the story, Edgar describes his looking upon a "few white trunks of decayed trees—with an utter depression of soul, which I can compare to no earthly sensation more properly than to the after-dream of the reveller upon opium—the bitter lapse into everyday life—the hideous dropping of the veil."

Never had such a house been created before! It lay upon "the precipitous brink of a black and lurid tarn." About the whole mansion and domain there was "an atmosphere which had no affinity with the air of heaven, but which had reeked up from the decayed trees, and the gray wall, and the silent tarn—a pestilent and mystic vapor, dull, sluggish, faintly discernible and leaden-hued."

The ancient house presented an odd, contradictory appearance. Although "minute fungi overspread the whole exterior, hanging in a fine tangled web-work from the eaves," the house itself was not dilapidated. The individual stones were in a "crumbling condition," but the parts still held together. But an observer could detect a "barely perceptible fissure, which, extending from the roof of the building in front, made its way down the wall in a zig-zag direction, until it became lost in the sullen waters of the tarn."

The visitor had come to spend several weeks with the proprietor of this decayed mansion, Roderick Usher, who had sent him a wild, appealing letter. The two had been boyhood friends, but now the changes in Roderick's appearance were startling. "Surely, man had never before so terribly altered, in so brief a period, as had Roderick Usher! It was with difficulty that I could bring myself to admit the identity of the wan being before me with the companion of my early boyhood."

As Edgar described Roderick, was he in reality describing himself?

A cadaverousness of complexion; an eye large, liquid, and luminous beyond comparison; lips somewhat thin and very pallid, but of a surpassingly beautiful curve; a nose of a delicate Hebrew model, but with a breadth of nostril unusual in similar formations; a finely moulded chin, speaking, in its want of prominence, of a want of moral energy; hair of a more than web-like softness and tenuity. . . .

The story's development brings forth the morbid themes Edgar loved to create: the lady Madeline's mysterious disease; her supposed death and the burial that followed; and the terrifying return from the family vaults. As Roderick shrieks, *"We have put her living in the tomb!"*, the enshrouded figure of the lady Madeline appears in the doorway. The climax of horror is reached in telling how she "fell heavily inward upon the person of her brother, and in her violent and now final death-agonies, bore him to the floor a corpse, and a victim to the terrors he had anticipated."

In describing a "mind haunted by phantoms—a disordered brain," Edgar inserted his poem, *The Haunted Palace,* in the center of the story. Here, the half-mad Roderick Usher recites a rhapsody about a valley once ruled by a kind and good king, whose inhabitants were uniquely happy. But "evil things" take control of the valley and bring a terrible change:

> And travellers now within that valley,
> Through the red-litten windows see
> Vast forms that move fantastically
> To a discordant melody;
> While, like a rapid ghastly river,
> Through the pale door,
> A hideous throng rush out forever,
> And laugh—but smile no more.

At the story's end, the zig-zag fissure that extends across the ancient house from roof to cellar breaks open; the mighty walls rush asunder and the "deep and dank tarn" closes over the fragments of the House of Usher.

In September, 1839, readers who opened the *Gentlemen's Magazine,* where they usually found conventional poems and light tales, must have been attracted by a story of a different type that was headed, in bold print, **The Fall of the House of Usher.** They soon learned to look for stories that carried the byline "Edgar A. Poe." In succeeding months Poe continued to contribute reviews, poems, and stories to the magazine, some of them reprints or revisions of earlier works. Now Edgar drew upon his never-ending store of memories to create the strange, dual character of William Wilson. From his happy childhood days in England, Edgar recreated the setting of the Manor House School at Stoke Newington. As always, he was acutely aware of the struggle between good and evil that takes place in every individual. The depraved William Wilson destroys his better self in a violent duel, and is in turn destroyed. He has lived only in his image— his conscience. The story *William Wilson,* sold to the *Gift,* an annual publication, was by their permission printed in the *Gentlemen's Magazine* October, 1839, issue.

For some time Edgar had been negotiating with Lea and Blanchard, Philadelphia publishers, for the printing of a collection of his stories. These included his early group, titled *Tales of the Folio Club,* which he had also referred to as *Eleven Tales of the Arabesque.* The terms "grotesque" and "arabesque," to Edgar, seemed to indicate the two classes of stories he had written. He had borrowed the words from an article by Walter Scott and proposed to use them for the title of his new collection.

Despite the recognition he had received from both the public and the critics, Lea and Blanchard were reluctant to print his tales. The agreement that was finally concluded made it plain that Edgar was to be paid nothing. The sad plight of a writer in the year 1839 is illustrated in the letter that dictated the terms of publication:

As your wish in having your Tales printed is not immediately pecuniary, we will at our own risque and expense print a Small Ed. say 1,750 copies. This sum if sold—will pay but a small profit which if realized is to be ours—The copyright will remain with you, and when ready a few copies for distribution among your friends will be at your Service.

Edgar had no choice but to agree to the terms offered by Lea and Blanchard. The two volumes, containing twenty-five stories, and titled *Tales of the Grotesque and Arabesque,* appeared at the end of the year. Within the volumes were all the stories Edgar had written, including such earlier ones as *Berenice, Metzengerstein, Morella,* and *A MS. Found in a Bottle.* Neither the critics nor the general readers were able to appreciate that these two books contained the best stories yet written by an American author.

Meanwhile, as in his days on the *Messenger,* Edgar maintained a steady correspondence with other authors, critics, and personal friends. In the hope of receiving some constructive comment, he sent copies of the *Gentlemen's Magazine* to Washington Irving. In comparing the story first published, *The Fall of the House of Usher,* with a later one, *William Wilson,* Irving wrote:

I could add for your private ear, that I think the last tale much the best, in regard to style. It is simpler. In your first you have been too anxious to present your picture vividly to the eye, or too distrustful to your effect, and have laid on too much coloring. It is erring on the best side—the side of luxuriance. . . .

Irving may have preferred the simplicity of *William Wilson,* but the passing years have demonstrated that what he described as "too much coloring" in the *House of Usher* was the very essence of Edgar's style—the Poe "trademark." With these splashes of color Edgar created the gloomy, foreboding atmosphere which thrilled countless readers.

Another of his correspondents was Dr. James Evan Snodgrass, of Baltimore, a man whose friendship Edgar valued highly. Snodgrass, a physician, had been an editor on the Baltimore *Visiter* and on the *Museum.*

During 1840, Edgar worked hard to make *Burton's* an outstanding literary magazine. But the cordial relationship between William Burton and himself was gradually changing. A number of disagreements arose: Burton was reluctant to give Edgar sufficient authority as editor, even though Edgar had undertaken most of the responsibility for the magazine. Burton felt that Edgar was not contributing enough of his own writings. On his own part, Edgar objected to a scheme of Burton's which involved the offering of premiums to authors. The premiums were cash awards, used as a competitive plan to encourage writers to contribute to the magazine. Edgar's contention was that the premiums scheme was dishonest. The quarrel between the two men grew in intensity, with feelings becoming quite bitter. Edgar's friend, Dr. Snodgrass, had evidently complained about the disappearance of an essay he had sent to the *Gentlemen's Magazine,* and in reply, on June 17, 1840, Edgar wrote:

Were I in your place I would take some summary method of dealing with the scoundrel, whose infamous line of conduct in regard to this whole Premium scheme merits, and shall receive exposure. I am firmly convinced that it was never his intention to pay one dollar of the money offered; and indeed his plain intimations to that effect, made to me personally and directly were the immediate reason of my cutting the connexion so abruptly as I did.

The "connexion" referred to was his position as editor, which Edgar gave up that same month. But other matters were also involved in the quarrel between the two. Without Edgar's knowledge, Burton had been advertising the *Gentlemen's Magazine* for sale. On his part, Burton accused Edgar of neglecting his duties on the magazine, and in the continuing quarrel, references were made to Edgar's drinking habits.

In a letter written to his friend, Dr. Snodgrass, Edgar referred to Burton's accusation and offered a vigorous denial of the charges, giving details to prove that he had *not* been drinking:

. . . You are a physician, and I presume no physician can have difficulty in detecting the *drunkard* at a glance. You are, moreover, a literary man, well read in morals. You will never be brought to believe that I could write what I daily write, as I write it, were I as this villain would induce those who know me not, to believe. In fine, I pledge you, before God, the solemn word of a gentleman, that I am temperate even to rigor.

Edgar then stressed that, from the first moment he took his position on the magazine up to the time he resigned, *nothing stronger than water had passed his lips.* He went on to explain,

At no period of my life was I ever what men call intemperate. I never was in the *habit* of intoxication. I never drank drams, &c. But, for a brief period, while I resided in Richmond, and edited the *Messenger* I certainly did give way, at long intervals, to the temptation held out on all sides by the spirit of Southern conviviality. My sensitive temperament could not stand an excitement which was an everyday matter to my companions. In short, it sometimes happened that I was completely intoxicated. For some days after each excess I was invariably confined to bed. But it is now quite four years since I have abandoned every kind of alcoholic drink—four years, with the exception of a single deviation, which occurred shortly *after* my leaving Burton, and when I was induced to resort to the occasional use of *cider,* with the hope of relieving a nervous attack.

Again, before the letter ended, Edgar wrote, "I have now only to repeat to you, in general, my solemn assurance that my habits are as far removed from intemperance as the day from the night. My sole drink is water."

Truth and sincerity appear evident in the explanation and candid confession of the few periods when he had been guilty of drinking. Events of the past and the future make clear that Edgar, throughout his life, drank only during short periods of illness, mental depression, and, as he indicated, during the occasional temptations of social affairs.

Another cause of conflict between the two men was based upon a private project to which Edgar devoted much of his spare time. He wished to edit and publish a literary journal of his own—one that he would control fully and completely. This was to become his lifelong dream. He had seen enough of magazines of poor literary quality that offered mediocre poetry and prose, whose editors feared to lose circulation by criticizing even the weakest writings.

To interest the public in his project, Edgar determined to prepare and mail a prospectus which explained his ideas. One day he sat at his desk and wrote, *Prospectus* of *The Penn Magazine, a Monthly Literary Journal*. . . .

The *Southern Literary Messenger* would be his guide, he thought, in certain respects. He recalled how hard he had tried to stamp his individuality on its pages. What must a high-quality publication have? He wrote the words, "a continuous definite character, and a marked certainty of purpose . . ." These are requisites.

He recalled his days at the *Messenger* and smiled. How critical he had been! "To those who remember the early days of the Southern periodical in question, it will be scarcely necessary to say that its main feature was a somewhat over-done causticity in its department of Critical Notices of new books."

Edgar would never lose the ability to look back at his youthful enthusiasms and understand and admit his mistakes. He recognized them but was not ashamed of them. Young writers and critics are bound to be impetuous—to arrive at opinions quickly and, on occasion, mistakenly. He wrote:

The *Penn Magazine* will retain this trait of severity insomuch only as the calmest yet sternest sense of justice will permit. Some years since elapsed may have mellowed down the petulance without interfering with the vigor of the critic.

What should the purposes and goals of the magazine be, he asked himself? His pen noted the phrases that occurred to him: "an honest and a fearless opinion . . . an absolutely independent criticism . . . a criticism . . . holding itself aloof from all personal bias . . ."

He frowned at the thought of the pressures to which the current magazines were yielding, and wrote again, referring to the "arrogance of those organized *cliques* which, hanging like nightmares upon American literature, manufacture, at the nod of our principal booksellers, a pseudo-public opinion by wholesale."

To complete the picture of his ideal magazine, he stated, "Its aim chiefly shall be *to please*—and this through means of versatility, originality, and pungency." Of course, the *Penn* would be without "any tincture of the buffoonery, scurrility, or profanity, which are the blemish of some of the most vigorous of the European prints."

In a final flourish, he informed the public that the *Penn Magazine* would appear on the first of each month, "and will form, half-yearly, a volume of about 500 pages. The price will be $5 per annum, payable in advance, or upon receipt of the first number, which will be issued on the first of March, 1841."

The prospectus was dated January 1, 1841, but a public notice announcing the scheduled publication of the *Penn* had already been placed in the *Philadelphia Saturday Chronicle* for June 13, 1840. But the typical problems of lack of employment and nervous illness forced him to delay any further action. The impossible perfection of his ideal magazine was part of his perpetual youth and dreaming. The writer who could create an entire fantasy world was not one to relinquish dreams. He held himself to severely high standards in his writing and expected the same of others. The uncompromising ideals, the visions, the dreams—these were the sources of his imagination and originality.

His association with *Burton's Gentlemen's Magazine* at an end, Edgar now began searching for a new position. Fortunately, the magazine was sold to George Rex Graham, owner of a smaller publication, the *Casket,* and he was anxious to retain Edgar's services. In April, 1841, Edgar became one of the editors of the new *Graham's Magazine.* But before making him a member of the staff, *Graham's* had arranged for the printing of one of Edgar's most unusual stories—*The Man of the Crowd.*

The great writer is always an observer of people—their faces, their actions, their gestures. Edgar had long possessed the powers of close observation, of concentration upon the smallest details. In his stories he chose to write in the first person so that he could be in the center of events, examining, probing, and analyzing. Sometimes he observed and reported every thought and movement of the main character; sometimes he *was* the main character, revealing his own mind: the fears, the evil drives, the strangely twisted desires. In *Berenice,* aware of his true habit of intense concentration, he exaggerated, and made himself the man with a *monomania,* which "consisted in a morbid irritability of those properties of the mind in metaphysical science termed the *attentive.*" This was his fantasy world, but in real life he was forever the man with the powers of mind called *the attentive.*

The Man of the Crowd provided him with a chance to demonstrate his unique quality of observation. "I sat at the large bow-window of the D—— Coffee-House in London," he wrote. ". . . I felt a calm but inquisitive interest in every thing." At first, he "looked at the passengers in masses"; but his natural curiosity could not be submerged. "Soon, however, I descended to details, and regarded with minute interest the innumerable varieties of figure, dress, air, gait, visage, and expression of countenance."

Now Edgar weighed and analyzed every type of individual. "The tribe of clerks was an obvious one. . . . There were the junior clerks of flash houses—young gentlemen with tight coats, bright boots, well-oiled hair, and supercilious lips. . . .

"The division of the upper clerks of staunch firms, or of the 'steady old fellows,'" he wrote, "it was not possible to mistake. These were known by their coats and pantaloons of black or brown, made to sit comfortably, with white cravats and waistcoats, broad solid-looking shoes, and thick hose or gaiters. They had all slightly bald heads, from which the right ears, long used to pen-holding, had an odd habit of standing off on end. . . ."

As he sits studying the passers-by, he sees "swell pickpockets," and gamblers who are easy to recognize in spite of their variety of dress, because "all were distinguished by a certain sodden swarthiness of complexion, a filmy dimness of eye, and pallor and compression of lip." Furthermore, these gamblers could always be identified by two other traits: "a guarded lowness of tone in conversation, and a more than ordinary extension of the thumb in a direction at right angles with the fingers."

Soon the main character appears on the scene. He is an old man who instantly arouses Edgar's interest. He is analyzed as one of many qualities, "of vast mental power, of caution, of penuriousness, of avarice, of coolness, of malice, of blood-thirstiness, of triumph, of merriment, of excessive terror, of intense—of supreme despair." Edgar stares and writes, "How wild a history," I said to myself, "is written within that bosom!"

He must follow this old man—must learn more about him. In thick humid fog and heavy rain he keeps on the man's trail, noting that he persists always in staying with the crowd. He is seized by panic as the hour grows late and the throngs begin to disappear from the streets. He finds his way to one of the principal theaters; the play is over and the audience is pouring out. "I saw the old man gasp as if for breath while he threw himself amid the crowd," Edgar writes.

Later the old man hurries to a slum area where "every thing wore the worst impress of the most deplorable poverty, and of the most desperate crime." Here he attempts to lose himself among the drunken, carousing revelers. Edgar follows him all through the night and the next day. Toward the end of his narrative he writes,

And, as the shades of the second evening came on, I grew wearied unto death, and, stopping fully in front of the wanderer, gazed at him steadfastly in the face. He noticed me not, but resumed his solemn walk, while I, ceasing to follow, remained absorbed in contemplation. "This old man," I said at length, "is the type and the genius of deep crime. He refuses to be alone. *He is the man of the crowd.* It will be in vain to follow; for I shall learn no more of him, nor of his deeds. . . ."

From the observer in *The Man of the Crowd,* whose sharp eyes and mind caught and analyzed every detail of human behavior, were to come the world's greatest stories of scientific deduction. In these Edgar would build the foundation for the modern story of crime and investigation—the detective story. None before him had seen its real possibilities: the creation of a great detective with analytical powers, who pursues every clue and uses brilliant logic and perception to solve the crime. The detective is C. Auguste Dupin, and he is the hero of Edgar's tales of *ratiocination*—of formal, step-by-step reasoning. The first of these, *The Murders in the Rue Morgue,* would appear in *Graham's* in April, 1841. Now Edgar's dazzling talent would branch into two directions: realistic tales of mystery or murder, stressing precise, unerring detection; and stories in a strange fantasy world of the warped human mind, terror and death.

10 · *The Detective Story*

Before assuming the position of editor for *Graham's Magazine,*
Edgar had already demonstrated a versatility which no other writer
had equaled. The variety of his writings was amazing: poetry,
book reviews, critical notes, essays, and stories. In subject matter,
he traveled at ease from his original world of fantasy to the precise,
penetrating area of literary criticism, to the brilliant statement of
new ideas and standards in his essays, or to the world of scientific
realism. In May, 1840, the *Gentlemen's Magazine* had even printed
his essay on the *Philosophy of Furniture,* in which he outlined
rules of good taste for interior decoration and gave a detailed
description of an ideal room.

Now, for the years 1841–1843, he was to specialize in the role
of super-detective. In the first part of *The Murders in the Rue
Morgue,* Edgar was really describing the processes of his own
mind:

As the strong man exults in his physical ability, delighting in such
exercises as call his muscles into action, so glories the analyst in that
moral activity which *distentangles.* . . . He is fond of enigmas, of
conundrums, hieroglyphics; exhibiting in his solutions of each a degree
of *acumen* which appears to the ordinary apprehension praeternatural.

Edgar went on to explain that "the analytical power should not
be confounded with simple ingenuity; for while the analyst is
necessarily ingenious, the ingenious man is often remarkably incapable of analysis."

With the launching of his bizarre murder mystery, he again
turns to the first person, becoming the observer who takes part
vicariously in the scientific investigations of the celebrated *Monsieur
C. Auguste Dupin.*

EXTRAORDINARY MURDERS—the evening paper blares
the startling news:

This morning, about three o'clock, the inhabitants of the Quartier
St. Roch were roused from sleep by a succession of terrific shrieks,
issuing, apparently, from the fourth story of a house in the Rue Morgue,
known to be in the sole occupancy of one Madame L'Espanaye, and
her daughter, Mademoiselle Camille L'Espanaye. . . .

The gendarmes found the apartment "in the wildest disorder.
. . . On a chair lay a razor, besmeared with blood. On the hearth

were two or three long and thick tresses of gray human hair, also dabbled with blood, and seeming to have been pulled out by the roots."

Madame L'Espanaye has vanished, but the corpse of her daughter is found, head downward, in the chimney. It had been "forced up the narrow aperture for a considerable distance." An examination disclosed that the face had "many severe scratches," and upon the throat were "dark bruises, and deep indentations of finger nails, as if the deceased had been throttled to death." Horror is now piled upon horror:

After a thorough investigation of every portion of the house without farther discovery, the party made its way into a small paved yard in the rear of the building, where lay the corpse of the old lady, with her throat so entirely cut that, upon an attempt to raise her, the head fell off. The body, as well as the head, was fearfully mutilated—the former so much so as scarcely to retain any semblance of humanity.

Monsieur Dupin and his observing companion eagerly read the next day's paper which contains the testimony of witnesses and of the physician who examined the bodies. Witnesses agreed that they had heard shrieks coming from the apartment, the sounds of angry voices, one shouting words in French or Italian, another speaking shrilly in a strange language. The physician and the surgeon were in agreement that the young woman had been strangled and that her mother may have been beaten to death with a club. Her throat had been slashed with a sharp instrument —probably a razor.

Edgar, as Dupin's shadow, acknowledges that the mystery seems insoluble. "I saw no means by which it would be possible to trace the murderer," he says.

Dupin is not at all discouraged. He offers a scathing criticism of the Parisian police procedures. "We must not judge of the means by this shell of an examination," he says. "The Parisian police, so much extolled for *acumen,* are cunning, but no more. There is no method in their proceedings, beyond the method of the moment. They make a vast parade of measures. . . ." He goes on in amused contempt to state that their results "are brought about by simple diligence and activity." Vidocq, the actual French Minister of Police, who has solved a number of crimes, is described insultingly as "a good guesser, and a persevering man . . . without educated thought. . . ."

The two men proceed to the Rue Morgue and to the dwelling

where the body of Mademoiselle L'Espanaye had been found. After a thorough examination of everything, Dupin puts his finger upon the one aspect of the crime which the police have not noted. He asks his companion if he has observed anything *"peculiar* at the scene of the atrocity." His companion is puzzled, but Dupin points out that the *outré,* or bizarre, nature of the crime should make it easy to solve. Voices had been heard in violent argument, yet nobody was discovered in the upstairs apartment other than the murdered woman. There was no way of leaving without being seen. How are we to start our investigations in this baffling situation? ". . . it should not be so much asked 'what has occurred,' as 'what has occurred that has never occurred before.' "

Dupin now begins a minute analysis of his clues. They are based upon the two windows in the chamber and include hidden springs, two nails, a lightning rod, and a swinging shutter. In rapid order his brilliant mind assembles and interprets other clues: the peculiar voice that was heard; the remarkable strength needed to thrust a body up the chimney; the great force needed to pull out the very thick tresses of human hair; and the fact that the tuft of hair found clutched in the woman's fingers was *not* human hair. The series of dark bruises on the throat, evidently impressions of fingers, are placed in a position that no human fingers can duplicate.

The detection was Dupin's but the scientific mind belonged to Edgar. He had already shown, as part of his remarkable background, his familiarity with Baron Georges Cuvier, the French naturalist, who had founded the science of palaeontology. He now drew upon this knowledge for Dupin's astonishing solution to the murders.

"Read this passage from Cuvier," Dupin instructs:

It was a minute anatomical and generally descriptive account of the large fulvous Ourang-Outang of the East Indian Islands. The gigantic stature, the prodigious strength and activity, the wild ferocity, and the imitative propensities of these mammalia are sufficiently well known to all. I understood the full horrors of the murder at once.

The next step is for Dupin to find the owner of the Ourang-Outang. His clues and further deductions make it clear that the owner is a man who has been a sailor on a Maltese vessel. When trapped by Dupin, he reveals that he allowed the Ourang-Outang to escape from his residence; the creature then made its way to the dwelling of Madame L'Espanaye, scaled the wall, and entered her chamber to commit the violent murders. An innocent man, Adolphe Le Bon, was released from custody. A bank clerk, he had helped carry two bags of money to the Espanaye apartment, an action which had caused him to fall under suspicion.

Edgar's imagination, ingenuity, and brilliance in scientific induction had led to a story in a new form. The skillful technique used in *The Murders in the Rue Morgue,* in which Edgar assembled the clues, described them painstakingly, but maneuvered so as to keep the reader in suspense and bafflement until the moment of solution, was his invention. The detective story, with its analytical approach, owes its existence to him, and from his mind and hands it has passed down to delight millions of readers in succeeding generations. In 1867, Emile Gaboriau, the French novelist, wrote *File No. 113,* emulating Edgar's Dupin with another invincible detective, Monsieur Lecoq. And without Auguste Dupin and his emphasis upon the "attentive," Sherlock Holmes, Watson and Baker Street might never have come into being! Certainly, as an observer and admirer of Dupin in *The Murders in the Rue Morgue,* Edgar set the stage for Watson, Holmes' continually amazed admirer. Holmes' readers will quickly identify one of Sherlock's favorite devices which Dupin used in 1841. He and his companion, strolling along a Paris street, had not "spoken a syllable for fifteen minutes at least." Then Dupin speaks suddenly, and a familiar scene takes place:

"He is a very little fellow, that's true, and would do better for the *Theatre des Varietes."*

"There can be no doubt of that," I replied, unwittingly, and not at first observing (so much had I been absorbed in reflection) the extraordinary manner in which the speaker had chimed in with my meditations.

Agape, Dupin's companion asks, "How was it possible you should know I was thinking of—Chantilly?" Dupin informs him of his exact reflections: "You were remarking to yourself that Chantilly's diminutive figure unfitted him for tragedy." At his request, Dupin reveals the method he used to read his friend's thoughts. The same ingenious analysis of clues was adopted by Holmes.

The detective Dupin, an analyst whose "results are brought about by the very soul and essence of method," was far too stimulating a creation to be allowed to vanish after solving a single murder case. Edgar had plans for him; he was to reappear in other stories of *ratiocination—The Mystery of Marie Roget* and *The Purloined Letter*.

Meanwhile, Edgar continued his daily duties as editor of *Graham's Magazine*. Early in 1840, he had moved with his family to a home on Coates Street, near the Schuylkill River. The offices of *Graham's* were some three miles away, at Third and Chestnut Streets. As he had done in the past with *Burton's,* Edgar was to devote every ounce of creative energy to his present position. But his disappointing experiences with popular publications, and above all, with their owners, had left him with few illusions. From the start he regarded *Graham's* as a temporary haven only. His plans to publish his own magazine, the *Penn,* could not be realized. In April, 1841, he had written to his friend Snodgrass, "The *Penn,* I hope, is only 'scotched, not killed.' . . ." His belief was that "The *Penn* project will unquestionably be resumed hereafter." He was, of course, mistaken; the *Penn* was dead. But dreams always occupied a corner of his imaginative mind. A vision of a new literary magazine, to be named *The Stylus,* was already taking shape.

Graham's Magazine had been launched with a subscription list of 5,000; in the next fourteen or fifteen months, with Edgar as editor, the list would rise to 40,000. George Rex Graham, the 27-year-old owner, was one who understood the value of publicity and knew how to appeal to popular taste. He was willing to gamble—to spend money liberally—in the belief that he had a formula for success. Authors with reputations were offered more money than any magazine had previously paid. Henry Wadsworth Longfellow was paid $50 or more for each of his poems; for his play, *The Spanish Student,* he received $150. James Fenimore Cooper was paid $1,000 for a group of his stories, and $1,800 for his novel, *Jack Tier.*

In the midst of this lavish spending, with engravings for the magazine costing up to $200 each and with unheard-of amounts being laid out for fancy paper, Edgar, as the one most responsible for the periodical's success, received only $800 a year—less than he had been paid on the *Messenger.* It was easy to understand why his impatience and bitterness should grow. In his editorial position he wrote regularly to distinguished authors and poets soliciting their creations for the pages of the magazine. On May 3, 1841, in writing to Longfellow, Edgar displayed his extreme modesty:

Mr. George R. Graham, proprietor of Graham's Magazine, a monthly journal published in this city and edited by myself, desires me to beg of you the honor of your contribution to its pages. . . . I confess that I have but little hope of inducing you to write for us,—and, to say truth, I fear that Mr. Graham would have opened the negotiation much better in his own person, for I have no reason to think myself favorably known to you; but the attempt was to be made, and I make it.

Edgar's modesty in not thinking himself "favorably known" to Longfellow is a reflection of a situation which must have driven him to the depths of discouragement and pessimism. In the years of his writing and editing, and in the genius of his creation, he had but touched the edge of fame—and fortune remained always beyond him. He was an envious bystander, watching the success of men whose talents and imagination could never match his.

Bitterness must have filled him as he wrote to Longfellow, "I should be overjoyed if we could get from you an article each month,—either poetry or prose,—length and subject *á discrétion*. In respect to terms, we would gladly offer you *carte blanche;* and the periods of payment should also be made to suit yourself." Longfellow was offered the privilege of writing on any subject he chose, at any price he demanded! Yet for one of his most famous stories, *The Gold Bug,* Edgar was paid the trivial sum of $52.

In his answer to Edgar, Longfellow exhibited kindness and consideration:

You are mistaken in supposing that you are not "favorably known to me." On the contrary, all that I have read from your pen has inspired me with a high idea of your power; and I think you are destined to stand among the first romance-writers of the country, if such be your aim.

Graham, in one important respect, was lenient and understanding with his talented editor: he knew about Edgar's hope of launching his own magazine, and appeared to have no objection to Edgar's promotion of the magazine in his spare time. To such distinguished authors as Longfellow, Cooper, Irving, and Halleck, Edgar wrote letters explaining his project for a literary publication of superior quality. On occasion he referred to "George R. Graham and myself" as the sponsors, although it seems clear that Graham, as owner of a financially successful magazine, had no real interest in another.

The stream of stories, essays, and poems continued to flow. In May, 1841, *Graham's* contained *A Descent into the Maelstrom,* a tale in which Edgar placed his exciting descriptions and scientific detail, while creating an atmosphere of terror. Again the first-person observer, he sits with his Norwegian guide atop a cliff, looking down at "a sheer unobstructed precipice of black shining rock, some fifteen or sixteen hundred feet from the world of crags" that lies below. They are on the Helseggen Mountain in the province of Nordland.

They watch the ocean begin to churn, "heaving, boiling, hissing —gyrating in gigantic and innumerable vortices." Small whirlpools form and then disappear; a frightening change takes place in the swirling waters as a vast circle of more than a mile in diameter appears before his eyes.

The edge of the whirl was represented by a broad belt of gleaming spray; but no particle of this slipped into the mouth of the terrific funnel, whose interior, as far as the eye could fathom it, was a smooth, shining and jet-black wall of water, inclined to the horizon at an angle of some forty-five degrees, speeding dizzily round and round with a swaying and sweltering motion, and sending forth to the winds an appalling voice, half shriek, half roar, such as not even the mighty cataract of Niagara ever lifts up in its agony to Heaven.

They are witnessing the furious motions of the "great whirlpool of the maelstrom," or, as the Norwegians call it, the *Moskoe-strom,* because its greatest violence occurs between the island of Moskoe and the coast.

The guide reveals that he has brought his companion here, not only to watch the maelstrom, but also to tell him the story of "six hours of deadly terror" which he had endured three years earlier. "You suppose me a *very* old man," he says, "—but I am not. It took less than a single day to change these hairs from a jetty black to white, to weaken my limbs, and to unstring my nerves . . ." From his lips comes the appalling tale of how he and his two brothers, owners of a "schooner-rigged smack of about seventy tons burthen," were caught in the whirl of the Strom, and made the headlong descent "into the abyss."

In *Graham's* for June, 1841, Edgar turned to a contemplation of the beauties of nature with the printing of *The Island of the Fay.* The tale of one of his "lonely journeyings" recalls his love of solitude during his ramblings in the Ragged Mountains near Charlottesville. He chances upon a "certain rivulet and island," and gives himself up to reverie and fanciful imaginings. "If ever island were enchanted," he says, "this is it. This is the haunt of the few gentle Fays who remain from the wreck of the race. . . ."

The image of his cherished Virginia appears once more in his tragic story, *Eleonora,* printed in the fall of 1841. Although Edgar had sold the story to the *Gift,* an annual, it was also published in the Boston *Nation* and the New York *Weekly Tribune.*

In the opening paragraph of *Eleonora,* Edgar speculates about madness. The question must have troubled him often—where is the dividing line between creative genius and madness? He wrote,

I am come of a race noted for vigor of fancy and ardor of passion. Men have called me mad; but the question is not yet settled, whether madness is or is not the loftiest intelligence—whether much that is glorious—whether all that is profound—does not spring from disease of thought—from *moods* of mind exalted at the expense of the general intellect.

He places himself, again, within a tale of the death of a beautiful woman, who "had seen that the finger of Death was upon her bosom." He was her lover, and her greatest anguish was that once she was entombed in the "Valley of the Many-Colored Grass," he would transfer the love which was "so passionately her own to some maiden of the outer and every-day world." He throws himself at her feet and makes a vow that he will never "bind himself in marriage to any daughter of Earth."

Later he breaks the vow, to marry the ethereal Ermengarde. But Eleonora, in keeping with the story's atmosphere of tenderness and understanding, forgives him, and in the silence of the night he hears her soft, sweet voice speaking to him:

Sleep in peace; for the Spirit of Love reigneth and ruleth, and, in taking to thy passionate heart her who is Ermengarde, thou art absolved, for reasons which shall be made known to thee in Heaven, of thy vows to Eleonora.

Unlike the somber, brooding mood of *Ligeia* and *Morella,* where the two women fiercely reject death and return from it to claim their lover, *Eleonora* ends in tranquillity and acceptance.

The pressure of his duties on *Graham's Magazine* and the hours spent on his own writings absorbed much of Edgar's energies, but at no time could he find a longed-for security in his work. He had learned through painful experience how difficult it was to earn an adequate living through writing and editing. As a result, when his friend Frederick W. Thomas, who had known

Henry Poe and had met Edgar in Philadelphia, wrote to him about the advantages of a government position, Edgar's interest was strong. Thomas had inquired temptingly,

. . . How would you like to be an office holder here at $1500 per year payable monthly by Uncle Sam, who, however slack he may be to his general creditors, pays his officials with due punctuality. How would you like it?

Thomas dwelled upon how little work there was, and explained how easy it would be for a person to spend his time on literary composition, or as he termed it, "if you choose to lucubrate in a literary way, why you can lucubrate."

Edgar heard that Thomas had been appointed to a government office, and wrote to congratulate him, saying, "From the bottom of my heart I wish you joy. . . . For my own part, notwithstanding Graham's unceasing civility and real kindness, I feel more & more disgusted with my situation. Would to God, I could do as you have done." The appointment could be secured only through President Tyler. Edgar asked Thomas, "Do you seriously think that an application on my part to Tyler would have a good result?"

On July 1, 1841, Thomas wrote to mention that the influence of John P. Kennedy, who was a member of the House of Representatives, might be helpful. He further suggested that Edgar come to Washington. Edgar's reply gave a disturbing picture of his situation and mental state:

I wish to God I could visit Washington—but the old story, you know —I have no money—not even enough to take me there, saying nothing of getting back. It is a hard thing to be poor—but as I am kept so by an honest motive I dare not complain.

. . . I would be glad to get almost any appointment—even a $500 one—so that I have something independent of letters for a subsistence. . . .

Edgar's next comment made it plain that writing was not a matter of mere inspiration, but an exacting, difficult business. "To coin one's brain into silver, at the nod of a master," he said, "is to my thinking, the hardest task in the world." He closed by urging Thomas to see Kennedy and obtain his help in securing the desperately needed appointment. But in the matter of regular income or permanent employment, his life pattern—or perhaps his luck— was unchangeable. The attempt to obtain a government position was doomed to failure, just as other quests for financial security had failed in the past.

The hope may have died painfully, but the new year brought a severe blow which drove past agonies from his mind. On an evening in January, 1842, Edgar sat relaxing with his family. As always, one of his greatest joys was in listening to Virginia sing. On this occasion he was especially pleased at Virginia's willingness to perform, because his cousins, the Herrings, were present.

Virginia stood in the parlor facing the guests, her fingers running quickly over the harp. Then she began to sing in her high, clear voice. Edgar leaned forward in his chair, his eyes mirroring the deep love he felt for her. Suddenly, the voice that soared through the room faltered and broke. Virginia's face contorted in pain, and while her audience gasped, a stream of blood ran from her throat. Edgar jumped up in an attempt to reach her as she collapsed on the floor. She was carried to a bed, and minutes later Edgar left to summon the family doctor.

The cause of the hemorrhage was obvious—she had ruptured a blood vessel in her throat. Something else was quite evident to the doctor. Virginia was in an advanced state of consumption; the hemorrhage, a familiar symptom, indicated the stage of the disease. In the first hours of her illness Edgar suffered a paralyzing scare, seized by the unbearable thought that she might die. But the blood vessel slowly healed, and Edgar breathed and hoped again.

From this day on, Virginia was to have only short periods of recovery. And his moments of happiness and optimism were to be timed with the days that his fragile young wife would show a spot of color in her white cheeks and reveal some of her old animation.

Some months earlier, in his task of writing book reviews for *Graham's* and other periodicals, Edgar had become interested in Charles Dickens' historical novel, *Barnaby Rudge*. Appearing serially, the novel excited the reader's interest through its ingredients of violence, melodrama, and a murder mystery. Edgar had always taken pride in his remarkable ability to solve puzzles and to provide ingenious solutions to problems of all types. With only eleven chapters of *Barnaby Rudge* available, Edgar proceeded to analyze the plan of the narrative, predict the incidents that would naturally follow, and detect the murderer. On March 10, 1841, the clever analysis appeared in the *Saturday Evening Post,* and almost a year later, in February, 1842, Edgar printed a longer version of the review in *Graham's*. His success in "out-guessing" Dickens gave him satisfaction, but the encounter with *Barnaby Rudge* provided him with something far more significant—the germ of an idea that would lead, years later, to his most famous creation.

In the Dickens novel, Reuben Haredale, a wealthy gentleman, is attacked by Rudge, his steward, who is after a large sum of money possessed by his master. Rudge murders Haredale and also an unfortunate gardener who is aware of his crime. Upon returning to his home, Rudge reveals the murder to his wife and orders her to escape with him. She refuses and falls to the ground. As he tries to pull her to her feet, she seizes his wrist, noticing, then, in horror, that her hand is stained with blood—the blood of the murdered man. Her husband flees the country alone. On the day after the murder Mrs. Rudge gives birth to a son, Barnaby. He is an idiot who carries a strange *red mark upon his wrist,* and from birth he possesses an overpowering horror of blood.

Edgar's interest had been held by the murder mystery, but a minor participant in the events proved the most fascinating to him. The simple Barnaby owned a pet raven named Grip who traveled on his master's back in a basket. At times the raven would croak the word, "Never say die!" To Edgar, the raven as a symbol offered possibilities which Dickens had neglected. About Barnaby Rudge Edgar wrote,

The raven, too, intensely amusing as it is, might have been made, more than we now see it, a portion of the conception of the fantastic Barnaby. Its croakings might have been *prophetically* heard in the course of the drama. Its character might have performed, in regard to that of the idiot, much the same part as does, in music, the accompaniment in respect to the air.

Edgar's rich imagination quickly conceived the raven as an ominous, croaking *prophet.* The image of the deathly black bird could never be forgotten from the moment it plagued his mind. Later, the "grim, ungainly, ghastly, gaunt, and ominous bird of yore" would perch on a bust in his study while he cried, "Prophet! Thing of evil!—prophet still, if bird or devil!—"

In March, 1842, on his American tour, Charles Dickens visited Philadelphia. Anxious to discuss writing with the famous novelist, Edgar wrote to him, sending the volumes of his *Tales of the Grotesque and Arabesque* and a copy of the review which had predicted the outcome of *Barnaby Rudge*. Dickens was reported to have been astonished at Edgar's perception, and to have exclaimed, "The man must be the devil!"

The two authors met at the United States Hotel, with Dickens showing much interest in Edgar's stories and poems. There was a second meeting, and Dickens promised to use his best efforts to obtain a British publisher for Edgar's works. Edgar heard nothing further about the matter and wrote to Dickens, who replied some months later. Dickens wrote, "I have mentioned it to publishers with whom I have influence, but they have, one and all, declined the venture. . . ." As in the past, Edgar's projects for recognition, which, despite repeated rejection, he tried over and over, were always blocked—always fated for failure.

The passing years had brought a maturity to Edgar's critical abilities. He began to state his ideas about poetry and prose with force and confidence. In April, 1842, his essay, *Longfellow's Ballads,* was printed in *Graham's*. Here, with an independence and honesty that few other critics possessed, he presented a severe criticism of Longfellow's poems. ". . . his conception of the *aims* of poesy is all *wrong*. . . . His didactics are all *out of place* . . ." Edgar commented that Longfellow had written brilliant poems *by accident,* when he permitted his genius "to get the better of his conventional habit of thinking. . . ."

He was criticizing a practice followed by other American poets who insisted upon teaching a *moral* in a poem—of turning poetry into an obvious sermon on good and evil, or in preaching spiritual values. In referring to Longfellow's poems, Edgar wrote, "We do not mean to say that a didactic moral may not be well made the *undercurrent* of a poetical thesis; but that it can never be well put so obtrusively forth, as in the majority of his compositions." In poetry, as in other forms of literature, Edgar was often far ahead of his time. He could see no reason for forcing trite moralisms into poetry, and modern poetic understanding has demonstrated that he was right, beyond all doubt.

In the same essay Edgar offered his classic definition of poetry: ". . . we would define in brief the Poetry of words as the *Rhythmical Creation of Beauty*. Beyond the limits of Beauty its province does not extend. Its sole arbiter is Taste. With the Intellect or with Conscience it has only collateral relations." Again he drove home the point: "It [poetry] has no dependence, unless incidentally, upon either Duty or *Truth*."

Unconcerned about the controversy stirred up by his blunt criticism, and the original standards he had devised for poetry, he continued to express his forceful opinions in a review of Hawthorne's *Twice Told Tales,* printed in *Graham's* in May, 1842. Here he lays down his rules concerning the length of a poem or narrative:

Were I bidden to say how the highest genius could be most advantageously employed for the best display of its own powers, I should answer, without hesitation—in the composition of a rhymed poem, not to exceed in length what might be perused in an hour. Within this limit alone can the highest order of true poetry exist.

Edgar granted that a poem should not be too short. "A poem *too* brief may produce a vivid, but never an intense or enduring impression." In the matter of length he next commented upon the "short prose narrative," of which he approved, defined as "requiring from a half-hour to one or two hours in its perusal." Edgar rejected the ordinary novel because of its excessive length. "As it cannot be read at one sitting," he said, "it deprives itself, of course, of the immense force derivable from *totality.*"

He then followed with his famous explanation of the *single effect* which must be the goal of the short story writer:

A skilful literary artist has constructed a tale. If wise, he has not fashioned his thoughts to accommodate his incidents; but having conceived, with deliberate care, a certain unique or single *effect* to be wrought out, he then invents such incidents—he then combines such events as may best aid him in establishing this preconceived effect.

Edgar felt strongly that everything hinged upon this *preconceived effect,* maintaining that, "If his very initial sentence tend not to the outbringing of this effect, then he has failed in his first step. In the whole composition there should be no word written, of which the tendency, direct or indirect, is not to the one pre-established design." It was natural that the short story, as viewed through his logical, analytical mind, should be a composition of precise organization.

In the spring of 1841, Edgar met a man who was to have a significant effect upon his life. The man was the Reverend Rufus Wilmot Griswold, a writer with little creative talent who had turned to editing anthologies. Eager to have his poems appear in Griswold's newest anthology, *Poets and Poetry of America,* Edgar arranged to meet Griswold. They became friends, and Griswold chose three of Edgar's poems, *The Coliseum, The Haunted Palace,* and *The*

Sleeper to include in his anthology. Edgar wrote a review of the collection for the *Boston Miscellany,* November, 1842, praising it generally, but criticizing the inclusion of poets whose works were "too mediocre to entitle them to more particular notice."

Edgar's dissatisfaction with his editorial position at *Graham's* finally drove him to the inevitable separation. On May 25, 1842, he wrote to his friend, Frederick Thomas, giving the full details, and mentioning that Rufus Griswold was taking his place:

The report of my having parted company with Graham is correct; although in the forthcoming June number there is no announcement to that effect; nor had the papers any authority for the statement made. My duties ceased with the May number. I shall continue to contribute occasionally. Griswold succeeds me.

Edgar offered his usual frank opinion of the magazine and its owner:

My reason for resigning was disgust with the namby-pamby character of the Magazine—a character which it was impossible to eradicate. I allude to the contemptible pictures, fashion-plates, music, and love-tales. The salary, moreover, did not pay me for the labour which I was forced to bestow. With Graham, who is really a very gentlemanly, although an exceedingly weak man, I had no misunderstanding.

The state of Virginia's illness is illustrated by Edgar's remark, "I am rejoiced to say that my dear little wife is much better, and I have strong hope of her ultimate recovery. . . ."

In the same month he returned to his atmosphere of terror and the supernatural to publish one of the most startling of his Arabesques. *The Masque of the Red Death,* a brief masterpiece of language and macabre effect, tells of the fearful plague that had spread throughout the country:

No pestilence had ever been so fatal, or so hideous. Blood was its Avatar and its seal—the redness and the horror of blood. There were sharp pains, and sudden dizziness, and then profuse bleeding at the pores, with dissolution.

But Prince Prospero had "summoned to his presence a thousand hale and light-hearted friends from among the knights and dames of his court," retiring to the seclusion of one of his abbeys. Elaborate plans were made for the safety of the Prince and his court. "A strong and lofty wall" with iron gates circled the abbey. All precautions were taken:

The courtiers, having entered, brought furnaces and massy hammers and welded the bolts. They resolved to leave means neither of ingress nor egress to the sudden impulses of despair or of frenzy from within. The abbey was amply provisioned. With such precautions the courtiers might bid defiance to contagion. The external world could take care of itself.

Inside the huge palace there was nothing but music, dancing, and gayety. "All these and security were within. Without was the 'Red Death.'" The Prince planned a masked ball of the "most unusual magnificence," to be held in the imperial suite of seven rooms, each decorated bizarrely in different colors, according to the Prince's tastes. The masked revelers thronged in all the chambers except the seventh, which was "shrouded in black velvet tapestries . . ." In this chamber also was a "gigantic clock of ebony. Its pendulum swung to and fro with a dull, heavy, monotonous clang." When the clock sounded on the hour it had "so peculiar a note" that the giddiest of the revelers "grew pale, and the more aged and sedate passed their hands over their brows as if in confused revery or meditation."

Among the dancers there appeared a masked figure whose "costume" caused murmurs "of terror, of horror, and of disgust."

The figure was tall and gaunt, and shrouded from head to foot in the habiliments of the grave. The mask which concealed the visage was made so nearly to resemble the countenance of a stiffened corpse that the closest scrutiny must have had difficulty in detecting the cheat. But the mummer had gone so far as to assume the type of the Red Death. His vesture was dabbled in *blood*—and his broad brow, with all the features of the face, was besprinkled with the scarlet horror.

The enraged Prince Prospero demands, "Who dares—who dares insult us with this blasphemous mockery? Seize him and unmask him—that we may know whom we have to hang at sunrise, from the battlements!"

But none dares to seize the frightful figure. The Prince alone pursues him to the black chamber and approaches him with drawn dagger. Moments later the Prince lies dead upon the carpet. And when the others summon courage to grasp the figure, they gasp "in unutterable horror at finding the grave cerements and corpselike mask, which they handled with so violent a rudeness, untenanted by any tangible form."

The Red Death had come like a thief in the night to claim them all. "And one by one dropped the revellers in the blood-bedewed halls of their revel, and died each in the despairing posture of his fall. . . . And Darkness and Decay and the Red Death held illimitable dominion over all."

In the year 1842, *The Masque of the Red Death* and others of Edgar's greatest stories were published in *Graham's Magazine*. But he did his writing while in the grip of an anguish he was unable to control. Virginia's ill health and the prospect of losing her had shaken him badly. The strain of the past years, the poverty and starvation—all had taken a heavy toll of his system. Now he existed from day to day in a world of agony and despair. Trapped in a web of seemingly insoluble problems, he turned once more to drink. His acquaintances deplored what they called his "irregularities," not understanding the sharpness of a pain that only drink could deaden. Nor were they capable of understanding the depth of his love for Virginia, and how the thought of her dying could turn his life into a nightmare.

The remaining years would see him reach the heights in the quality and popularity of his writing. But in his mental and physical health the decline had already begun. Whatever strength remained would be sacrificed to the goddess of creativity. She would give him a brief measure of success in exchange.

II · *More Detection, Cryptograms, and* The Gold Bug

"I need scarcely tell you," said Dupin, as he finished the perusal of my notes, "that this is a far more intricate case than that of the Rue Morgue; from which it differs in one important respect. This is an *ordinary,* although an atrocious, instance of crime. There is nothing peculiarly *outré* about it."

Once more the near-clairvoyant Monsieur C. Auguste Dupin is called upon to solve a murder case. His intended retirement, after his brilliant investigations in *The Murders in the Rue Morgue,* had been abruptly canceled. Evidently, his ingenious confrère, Edgar Allan Poe, who listened respectfully to his astonishing deductions, was reluctant to allow Monsieur Dupin to vanish from the scene after only one performance. It was time for another detective story. The incidents of a true murder mystery, the death of Mary Cecilia Rogers, tossed about in Edgar's mind until he was driven to writing about them.

In August, 1841, the body of Mary Rogers, a clerk, was found in the Hudson River. Her death caused excited comment and speculation, but more than a year later, when Edgar chose to use the circumstances in a story, the mystery remained unsolved. The newspapers appeared to agree that the murder had been committed by a gang of ruffians. Through his master-detective Dupin, Edgar proceeded to prove that this theory was wrong.

In writing his story, Edgar changed the setting from New York to Paris, renamed the girl Marie Roget, and made her a Parisian *grisette,* or shop girl. Early in the story he explains that, in *The Murders in the Rue Morgue,* his object had been "to depict some very remarkable features in the mental character of my friend, the Chevalier C. Auguste Dupin . . ." It did not occur to him that he should ever "resume the subject."

Marie Roget, a lovely 22-year-old girl, worked for Monsieur Le Blanc, a perfumer. On one occasion she disappeared for a week, but returned safely, just when the police were about to start investigations. Those who were curious could obtain no definite information as to where she had been. Marie left the shop to stay at home with her mother. Some months later she again disappeared for a period of three days; on the fourth day her corpse was found floating in the Seine River.

Dupin, in analyzing the various newspaper reports, concludes, as usual, that the police have overlooked much of the important evidence. They have failed to understand that there is an obvious connection between the first and second disappearances of Marie. The first episode makes it clear that a gang is not involved. Marie had eloped with a lover, a quarrel had followed, and she had returned home. Her secret lover, or betrayer, persuaded her to meet him again, and this time the murder took place. Dupin, merely by assembling the printed facts, finds the evidence to support his theory. Traces of a struggle have been found near a thicket at the Barriere du Roule. These very "traces," says Dupin, rule out any idea of a gang. They demonstrate "the absence of a gang." He asks, "What *struggle* could have taken place—what struggle so violent and so enduring as to have left its 'traces' in all directions—between a weak and defenceless girl and a *gang* of ruffians imagined? The silent grasp of a few rough arms and all would have been over."

Dupin further inferred that the girl's frock had not been torn accidentally in a struggle, but that a strip had been *purposely* ripped from the dress. The murderer used it to form a *bandage* or *handle* to carry the body. This in itself indicated that only *one* man was involved; a gang would have no need for a device of this sort.

By the time he had completed his analysis, Dupin had established some startling conclusions: the murderer, Marie's lover or secret associate, is "of swarthy complexion. This complexion, the 'hitch' in the bandage, and the 'sailor's knot' with which the bonnet-ribbon is tied, point to a seaman. His companionship with the deceased—a gay but not an abject young girl—designates him as above the grade of the common sailor." Dupin now recalled the report in the newspaper *Le Mercure,* which mentioned the fact that before her first absence Marie had spent much time with a young naval officer. All the evidence, Dupin believed, indicated that he was the guilty man.

The Mystery of Marie Roget was originally published in *Snowden's Ladies' Companion* for November and December, 1842, and February, 1843; but in a later printing Edgar added footnotes containing information that in his opinion *proved* the truth of a solution that he had deduced "at a distance from the scene of the atrocity, and with no other means of investigation than the newspapers afforded." He insisted that "the confessions of *two* persons, made at different periods, long subsequent to the publication, confirmed, in full, not only the general conclusion, but absolutely *all* the chief hypothetical details by which that conclusion was attained."

Years later, in a letter to his friend George W. Eveleth, Edgar explained:

The "naval officer" who committed the murder (or rather, the accidental death arising from an attempt at abortion) *confessed* it; and the whole matter is now well understood—but, for the sake of relatives, this is a topic on which I must not speak further.

At the end of 1842, Edgar's imagination became centered in strange themes of torture and of the mind haunted by a compulsion to commit an evil deed. The stories, *The Pit and the Pendulum* and *The Tell-Tale Heart,* were among his finest creations of terror and suspense.

In *The Pit and the Pendulum,* Edgar becomes the man under the "dread sentence of death" pronounced by the "black-robed judges" of the Inquisition. Even while confined in a black dungeon, his curiosity and logical mind lead him to investigate, and, by counting his paces as he walks, to estimate the size and shape of his prison. In the darkness he trips over the torn hem of his robe, falls to the floor, and discovers that he is on the brink of a pit. Only his timely accident has prevented him from taking another step, which would have tumbled him to a certain death. Upon awakening later, he finds himself strapped to a low platform, able to move only his head and left arm. A horde of rats descends upon him, attracted by the scent of meat in his earthen dish. He tries to scare them away, but at the same time becomes aware of a huge pendulum which is sweeping back and forth above him.

The sweep of the pendulum had increased in extent by nearly a yard. As a natural consequence its velocity was also much greater. But what mainly disturbed me was the idea that it had perceptibly *descended.* I now observed—with what horror it is needless to say—that its nether extremity was formed of a crescent of glittering steel, about a foot in length from horn to horn; the horns upward, and the under edge evidently as keen as a razor.

The pendulum creeps downward, and he realizes that its razor-sharp edge will soon cut across his robe. The idea comes to him to rub some particles of food over the bandage with which he is tied, to entice the rats to chew through the material. Edgar pictured their actions:

They pressed—they swarmed upon me in ever accumulating heaps. They writhed upon my throat; their cold lips sought my own; I was half stifled by their thronging pressure; disgust, for which the world has no name, swelled my bosom, and chilled, with a heavy clamminess, my heart.

The bandage loosens and he is free. But there are more ingenious tortures planned. He is saved only at the last moment by the entrance of the French army into the city.

In *The Pit and the Pendulum,* while Edgar had devised his usual inventive plot, the effect he was seeking was psychological—the overwhelming fear that gripped the prisoner must be made apparent through his mental agony.

There were very few happenings in the literary field that escaped Edgar's notice, and in November, 1842, he learned that James

Russell Lowell was founding a new monthly magazine, *The Pioneer*. Edgar wrote to inquire "whether some arrangement might not be made by which I should become a regular contributor." Lowell answered with enthusiasm, indicating, above all, that he wanted stories. He was fortunate in receiving one of Edgar's finest, which for personal reasons had been rejected by another publication. When the first number of *The Pioneer* appeared in January, 1843, it contained *The Tell-Tale Heart*. Here, with consummate skill, Edgar portrays the madman who cannot believe he is mad. Again, the author takes the first person role in his tale of horror:

TRUE!—nervous—very, very, dreadfully nervous I had been and am! but why *will* you say I am mad? The disease had sharpened my senses—not destroyed—not dulled them. Above all was the sense of hearing acute.

In *Berenice* Edgar shaped a mental sickness based upon a morbid irritability of the *attentive*—a concentration upon details that led to a frenzied desire for "thirty-two small, white, and ivory-looking substances . . . !" The sickness in *The Tell-Tale Heart* was of hearing—of an imagined acute hearing, and with it a monomania about an old man's evil eye:

. . . I loved the old man. He had never wronged me. He had never given me insult. For his gold I had no desire. I think it was his eye! yes, it was this! One of his eyes resembled that of a vulture—a pale blue eye, with a film over it. Whenever it fell upon me, my blood ran cold; and so by degrees—very gradually—I made up my mind to take the life of the old man, and thus rid myself of the eye for ever.

Every night he stealthily turns the latch of the old man's door, opens it, and peers in, holding a lantern so that "a single thin ray fell upon the vulture eye." But he cannot murder the man because he finds the eye closed: ". . . it was not the old man who vexed me, but his Evil Eye."

Edgar, as one who had endured suffering and pain in his own life, was able to picture vividly the mental anguish of others. The old man hears a noise at his door in the middle of the night and springs up in bed, crying, "Who's there?" Edgar describes the emotion of fear:

Presently I heard a slight groan, and I knew it was the groan of mortal terror. It was not a groan of pain or of grief—oh no!—it was the low stifled sound that arises from the bottom of the soul when over-charged with awe. I knew the sound well. Many a night, just at midnight, when all the world slept, it has welled up from my own bosom, deepening, with its dreadful echo, the terrors that distracted me.

Soon Edgar returns to his main theme: "And now have I not told you that what you mistake for madness is but over-acuteness of the senses?" He hears a "low, dull, quick sound, such as a watch makes when enveloped in cotton. . . . *It was the beating of the old man's heart.*"

Again, after he has killed the old man and hidden his dismembered corpse under the floor, he hears the same *"low, dull, quick sound."* The police have come to investigate, and they sit by, chatting pleasantly and smiling. He cannot believe that they do not hear the beating heart. They are "making a mockery" of his horror. As the heart beats louder, he shrieks, ". . . I admit the deed!—tear up the planks!—here, here!—it is the beating of his hideous heart!"

Within the framework of his stories of terror were always the strangely twisted minds and the evils of human nature, sadism, hatred, and passionate violence. Through his own struggles and mental turmoil Edgar had become aware of the *irrational*—the uncontrollable thoughts and actions, the illogical changes that seemed to spring from nowhere. From personal experience he had known some of these irrational acts to be caused by drinking and the use of drugs. The evil half of the dual William Wilson took part in debaucheries where "the wine flowered freely, and there were not wanting other and perhaps more dangerous seductions . . ." In *The Fall of the House of Usher,* Roderick's voice was described as "that leaden, self-balanced, and perfectly modulated guttural utterance, which may be observed in the lost drunkard, or the irreclaimable eater of opium, during the periods of his most intense excitement."

In Edgar's famous story, *The Black Cat,* the startling changes that occur in a man are caused, first of all, by drink—"through the instrumentality of the Fiend Intemperance." He writes, "I grew, day by day, more moody, more irritable, more regardless of the feelings of others." He begins to mistreat his wife and his animal pets, and as his disease grows upon him, "for what disease is like Alcohol!", he even turns upon the cat Pluto, his favorite playmate, to "deliberately cut one of its eyes from the socket!"

His drinking continues, driving him toward other sadistic deeds.

With the excesses of liquor comes a strange force that drives man toward irrational behavior—a force that Edgar chose to speculate about. It is the *spirit of perverseness*. He states,

Of this spirit philosophy takes no account. Yet I am not more sure that my soul lives, than I am that perverseness is one of the primitive impulses of the human heart. . . . Who has not, a hundred times, found himself committing a vile or stupid action, for no other reason than because he knows he should *not*?

In trying to account for the personal failings that had plagued him, is Edgar blaming this *spirit of perverseness?* He describes it as "this unfathomable longing of the soul *to vex itself*—to offer violence to its own nature." Like the characters in his stories, he was one who faced an accusing, punishing conscience. Often crushed by the feelings of his own guilt, he looked for ways to explain his weaknesses. In insisting that the individual is powerless to oppose the "primitive impulse" of *perverseness,* he may have been trying to excuse his own irrational acts.

The Black Cat was published on August 19, 1843, in the *United States Saturday Post*. But during the summer months, Edgar, as usual, had his hand in various creations, beginning new stories and revising and shaping old ones. Once more he became interested in mystery and the deductive processes—the story of *ratiocination*. This time he chose to exhibit his skill in a field that had always fascinated him—the field of cryptography.

In his longest work, *The Narrative of A. Gordon Pym,* Edgar experimented with a strange set of hieroglyphics derived from the shape of chasms that the wanderers encountered on a savage Antarctic island. The odd figures, according to Edgar, resembled Ethiopian and Arabic roots.

He had always taken great pride in his ability to solve cryptograms. For *Alexander's Weekly Messenger* of December 18, 1839, he had written an article titled, "Enigmatical and Conundrum-ical." On a momentary inspiration, he ventured to make a boasting claim; he hurled a challenge to his readers. The words might just as well have been,

> I CAN SOLVE ANY CIPHER OR CRYPTO-
> GRAM THAT IS SENT TO THIS PAPER.
> SEND THEM—ONE AND ALL! I CANNOT BE
> STUMPED!

The readers took up the challenge; he was deluged with cryptograms. One hundred of them poured in, and Edgar, not at all dismayed, set to work to find the solutions. He later claimed that he had solved all but one. In April, 1841, for *Graham's Magazine,* he returned to his favorite mental exercise, and challenged his readers once more. He had written about cryptograms in a foreign language; now he proposed to his audience that "Anyone who will take the trouble, may address us a note, in the same manner as here proposed, and the key phrase may be either in French, Italian, Spanish, German, Latin or Greek (or in any of the dialects of these languages), and we pledge ourselves for the solution of the riddle. The experiment may afford our readers some amusement—let them try it." Edgar, supremely confident, had offered to solve cryptograms in *six* foreign languages! This time, however, there was little response; only two cryptograms were received, and in the July issue of *Graham's* he printed them and revealed the solutions. Cryptograms continued to be his topic for several months, and he maintained his standing offer to solve any that were sent in.

The fascination for cryptograms remained with him, and in 1843 led to the writing of the most ingenious of his *Tales of Ratiocination—The Gold Bug.* Here the invincible Dupin is not the main character. The deductions are performed by William Legrand, and, as usual, Edgar is on the scene, sharing in the exciting adventure. For his setting Edgar returns to his Army days and his recollections of Sullivan's Island. The island, with its "scant, dwarfish" vegetation, becomes the residence of William Legrand and the spot where a treasure hunt occurs.

In the story, Edgar visits his old friend on the island, to discover that Legrand has found an unusual beetle of a brilliant gold color, "about the size of a large hickory nut—with two jet black spots near one extremity of the back, and another, somewhat longer, at the other." Legrand becomes mysteriously excited over a scrap of paper containing his sketch of the bug. Later events reveal that the supposed paper is really parchment, found by Legrand's Negro servant Jupiter near the same spot where the gold bug was discovered. When the parchment is held accidentally near the fire, a skull or death's-head appears, and upon being held to the fire again by Legrand, a cipher, "rudely traced, in a red tint," can be clearly read.

Edgar has now established the situation which will permit him to display his ingenuity. Through his character Legrand, who finds the cryptogram easy, having "solved others of an abstruseness ten thousand times greater," Edgar proceeds to offer an example of his faultless reasoning powers. The cryptogram is without letters, containing only numbers and punctuation marks. How are we to tell which letters are represented? The answer becomes obvious: of the characters in the cryptogram, the number 8 appears more frequently than the others—a total of thirty-three times. Since we are dealing with the English language, the number 8 must stand for the letter e, which occurs the most often. Once this is proved, the other letters fall easily into place.

The directions given in the cryptogram lead Legrand, his companion, and his servant Jupiter to a huge tree. On its seventh limb a bleached skull is perched. The gold bug has been fastened at the end of a string, and upon climbing the tree, Jupiter is instructed to drop the gold bug through the eye of the skull while holding fast to the string. After a first blunder by Jupiter in choosing the wrong eye, the dangling string gives them the location they are seeking. Buried beneath a mass of human bones, they find a huge chest containing the treasure of Captain Kidd.

Edgar had accepted $52 from George Graham for *The Gold Bug;* this was before learning of the *Dollar Newspaper's* short story contest. Graham obligingly agreed to return the story. The prize was $100, and from the moment *The Gold Bug* was submitted, it was an assured winner. The story was published on June 21 and 28, 1843, and, because of its popularity, was reprinted, not only in the *Dollar Newspaper,* but in the *Saturday Courier* as well.

The astonishing creativity of the year 1843 was carried on by a man who fought to sustain a hope that his Virginia would recover her health. In the passing months there was no recurrence of the hemorrhage which had carried her close to death. Although she remained an invalid, weakened often by periods of fever and coughing, Edgar was grateful for her partial recovery. But a year after the original rupture the blood vessel broke again. Once more she appeared to be dying, and Edgar spent his days in fear and hopelessness. Again, despair overcame him and he turned to drink. The crisis passed and Virginia seemed to be improving, but it was evident that she would never be permanently cured.

Attempts to find a publisher for his *Phantasy Pieces,* a collection of thirty-six stories, including the original twenty-five contained in *Tales of the Grotesque and Arabesque,* were unsuccessful, and in 1843 Edgar made plans to have them printed in a pamphet series. Only one pamphlet was printed; it contained two stories, *The Murders in the Rue Morgue* and *The Man That Was Used Up*. Published by William H. Graham, the pamphlet sold for 12½ cents!

In spite of Virginia's poor health and his own periods of illness, there was something in Edgar's nature that would not allow him to surrender—that drove him doggedly toward his goal of recognition. He had never given up his project for a literary magazine. In January, 1843, he had arranged with Thomas C. Clarke, publisher of the *Saturday Museum,* and Felix Darley, an illustrator, to join him in the publication of a magazine he had named *The Stylus.* Later he prepared a prospectus of *The Stylus* which stated that it was replacing the suspended *Penn Magazine. The Stylus,* scheduled to appear in July, 1843, would have a subscription price of five dollars annually, and would contain what was described as an "important feature"—*Critical and Biographical Sketches of American Writers.*

The *Saturday Museum* printed a long, flattering biography of Edgar, and later, his prospectus of *The Stylus.* With Clarke, the *Museum's* publisher, backing the magazine project and willing to supply part of the expenses, it was decided that Edgar should make a trip to Washington. His purpose in going was to secure subscriptions for *The Stylus* and to gain an audience with President Tyler or one of his assistants, in the hope of obtaining a government appointment. He left Philadelphia early in March, planning, upon his arrival in Washington, to seek the help of his friend, Frederick Thomas. On March 11th, he wrote to Clarke admitting that he had done nothing and explaining why:

My friend Thomas, upon whom I depended, is sick. I suppose he will be well in a few days. In the meantime I shall have to do the best I can. I have not seen the President yet.

While complaining that his expenses were more than he thought they would be (and asking Clarke to send ten dollars), he wrote, "I have got the subscriptions of *all* the Departments—President, &c I believe that I am making a *sensation* which will tend to the benefit of the Magazine." He added, "Day after tomorrow I am to lecture."

Unfortunately, certain events destroyed a promising beginning and forced a change of plans. In several evenings spent with J. E. Dow, Edgar allowed himself to drink too freely. Dow's letter to Clarke explained the circumstances:

He [Edgar] arrived here a few days since. On the first evening he seemed somewhat excited, having been over-persuaded to take some Port wine.

On the second day he kept pretty steady, but since then he has been, at intervals, quite unreliable.

. . . Under all the circumstances of the case, I think it advisable for you to come on and see him safely back to his home. Mrs. Poe is in a bad state of health, and I charge you, as you have a soul to be saved, to say not one word to her about him until he arrives with you. . . .

In sympathy and understanding, Dow wrote, "Mr. Poe has the highest order of intellect, and I cannot bear that he should be the sport of senseless creatures who, like oysters, keep sober, and gape and swallow everything."

Clarke did not come to Washington. Edgar returned home alone and was met at the train by his aunt. On March 16th, he wrote a long apologetic letter to Thomas and Dow. He promised to pay back the money he had borrowed from them. While he spoke jokingly, it was evident that he felt deeply ashamed over his conduct:

. . . Please express my regret to Mr. Fuller for making such a fool of myself in his house, and say to him (if you think it necessary) that I should not have got half so drunk on his excellent Port wine but for the rummy coffee with which I was forced to wash it down.

In referring wistfully to the hope that Robert Tyler, the President's oldest son, was still attempting to get him an inspectorship, Edgar said, ". . . I am as serious as a judge—& much more so than many. I think it would be a feather in Mr. Tyler's cap to save from the perils of mint julep—& 'Port wines'—a young man of whom all the world thinks so well & who thinks *so* remarkably well of himself."

Again, all the evidence indicated that Edgar, because of his temperament and nervous disposition, was strongly affected by small quantities of liquor. A note from Frederick Thomas explained Edgar's peculiar reaction to even the mildest of beverages:

. . . I have seen a great deal of Poe, and it was his excessive and at times marked sensibility which forced him into his "frolics," rather than any mere morbid appetite for drink, but if he took one glass of weak wine or beer or cider, the Rubicon of the cup was passed with him, and it almost always ended in excess and sickness.

Thomas, who knew Edgar from intimate association, said that "the accounts of his derelictions" . . . "were very much exaggerated. I have seen men who drank bottles of wine to Poe's wine-glasses who yet escaped all imputations of intemperance." Thomas stressed that Edgar possessed *"one of those temperaments whose only safety is in total abstinence.* He suffered terribly after any indiscretion."

Misfortune continued to follow him. On March 24, 1843, James Russell Lowell wrote to tell Edgar that the newly launched magazine *The Pioneer* was about to discontinue publication. He apologized for his inability to pay Edgar for his writings. That Edgar could ignore his desperate need for money, to write a letter of sympathy and understanding to Lowell, is an indication of the depth of his character. He was "deeply grieved" at Lowell's misfortune, and at the thought that Lowell should feel an apology was necessary. "As for the few dollars you owe me," he wrote, "—give yourself not one moment's concern about *them.* I am poor, but must be very much poorer, indeed, when I even think of demanding them." This kind of generosity and self-sacrifice comes only from those who have lived with poverty.

In April, 1844, *A Tale of the Ragged Mountains* appeared in *Godey's Lady's Book.* Here Edgar returned to his days at the University of Virginia when his solitary rambles took him into the mountains whose "delicious aspect of dreary desolation" he never forgot. In this setting he created the strange tale of Augustus Bedloe, who in a vision returns to the India of 1870 for a scene of violence.

But Edgar, troubled for some time over the vanishing opportunities in Philadelphia, faced the need for a decision. He could see little reason for remaining where he was; without steady employment, and with no chance of having his works published, it appeared to him that in Philadelphia his literary activities had come to a dead end. On April 6th, accompanied only by Virginia, he boarded a train for Perth Amboy where a steamer waited to take him to his destination—New York City.

He and Virginia arrived safely the next day, and, in a letter to his aunt, Edgar reported happily that "Sissy coughed none at all." After describing the generous portions of food served at their boarding house, Edgar again spoke of Virginia: "Sis is delighted, and we are both in excellent spirits. She has coughed hardly any and had no night sweat." Concerning himself he said, "I feel in excellent spirits & haven't drank a drop—so that I hope soon to get out of trouble." He promised his aunt that, as soon as he could "scrape together enough money," he would send it to her.

Facing the problem of supporting Virginia and himself in a new city, Edgar proceeded immediately to contact a New York publisher. The story he had for sale was most unusual. Perhaps he believed that, in order to make an impression in the great metropolis, he needed something sensational. It must be something that would focus public attention upon him—a means of instant publicity.

As he walked into the office of the *New York Sun,* he found it difficult to keep from chuckling to himself. The manuscript he carried with him contained one of the most hilarious practical jokes ever conceived by an author! It is hard to realize that the melancholy writer of tales of madness, torture, and death was capable of creating an amusing hoax that would fool thousands of *Sun* readers.

The newspaper's publisher, who was aware of Edgar's reputation, scanned the opening of the manuscript and turned, with raised eyebrows, to gaze at its author. The humorous light in Edgar's eyes, and the grin that he couldn't repress, puzzled the publisher, but he resumed his reading. Soon a broad smile spread over his face and then he burst out laughing. "Magnificent!" he said. "The *Sun* will print this—and as quickly as possible."

Edgar beamed happily and murmured his thanks.

"We'll run a special announcement in the Saturday morning issue," the publisher said. "And your story will appear in an extra!"

On Saturday morning, April 13th, the square around the *Sun* building was jammed with an excited throng whose babbling voices could be heard blocks away. They had either heard the astonishing news or had read the *Sun's* announcement and were waiting for the extra. At noon it finally appeared, and copies were sold to the crowd who snatched them from the vendors' hands and fought for possession of them. Readers could not miss the headlines printed in bold capitals:

ASTOUNDING NEWS! BY EXPRESS VIA NORFOLK! THE ATLANTIC CROSSED IN THREE DAYS! Signal Triumph of Mr. Monck Mason's **FLYING MACHINE!** Arrival at Sullivan's Island near Charleston, S.C. of Mr. Mason, Mr. Robert Holland, Mr. Henson, Mr. Harrison Ainsworth, and four others, in the Steering Balloon "Victoria" —After a passage of Seventy-Five Hours From Land to Land!

The fascinated reader whose eyes dropped to the story beneath the headlines read that "The great problem is at length solved! The air, as well as the earth and the ocean, has been subdued by science, and will become a common and convenient highway for mankind. *The Atlantic has been actually crossed in a Balloon!"*

In a learned manner, using the weighty language of science, Edgar presented the details of the voyage. First came a description of the balloon, and here Edgar drew upon his great store of scientific information to picture the balloon's dimensions and construction. He detailed its length, the number of cubic feet of gas it carried, the operations of its screw, and its procedure in ascending. The journal of the actual voyage began with *Saturday, April the 6th*. On that morning the balloon, moored in a courtyard at Penstruthal, North Wales, was inflated, set free, and was soon on its way.

Hardly any difficulties were encountered. On Sunday, the 7th, the journal stated that "crossing the ocean in a balloon is not so difficult a feat after all." On Tuesday, the 9th, the journal entry heralded the success: *"We are in full view of the low coast of South Carolina. The great problem is accomplished. We have crossed the Atlantic—fairly and easily crossed it in a balloon! God be praised! Who shall say that anything is impossible hereafter?"*

The crowd digested the story in a fever of excitement and ran to carry the incredible news everywhere. The impressive scientific details, and the realistic account of the preparations and the voyage, made the story appear to be genuine. Not until hours later did many of the readers understand that they had been fooled. The voyage across the Atlantic was a clever hoax! The entire story was Edgar's creation. Once before he had written a pseudo-scientific jest in the *Adventures of Hans Pfaall;* above all, he relished writing with all the scientific accuracy he could muster in order to give an air of realism to an absurd, impossible situation.

In a later edition of his stories, Edgar prefaced *The Balloon-Hoax* with a tongue-in-cheek remark:

The rush for the "sole paper which had the news" was something beyond even the prodigious; and, in fact, if (as some assert) the "Victoria" *did* not absolutely accomplish the voyage recorded, it will be difficult to assign a reason why she *should* not have accomplished it.

He must have obtained an additional chuckle through locating the balloon's destination at Sullivan's Island, a spot so remote to others and so familiar to him—the site for Captain Kidd's treasure in *The Gold Bug.*

In the *Columbia Spy,* on May 25, 1844, Edgar offered more comments. The furor of the *The Balloon-Hoax* undoubtedly supplied him with a ready outlet for his remarks:

. . . On the morning of its announcement, the whole square surrounding the "Sun" building was literally besieged, blocked up—ingress and egress being alike impossible, from a period soon after sunrise until about two o'clock P.M. . . . I never witnessed more intense excitement to get possession of a newspaper. As soon as the few first copies made their way into the streets, they were bought up, at almost any price, from the newsboys, who made a profitable speculation beyond doubt.

In the frenzied rush for papers, Edgar reported that he "saw a half-dollar given, in one instance, for a single paper, and a shilling was a frequent price." He said, "I tried, in vain, during the whole day, to get possession of a copy."

Only a week after his arrival in New York he had achieved a publicity which the publishers of the large city could interpret as a notice that a writer of originality and imagination was in their midst. *The Balloon-Hoax* was only a minor piece of writing, but it had served its purpose. Already sounding in the recesses of Edgar's mind were the croakings of a plaintive bird. When the "ebony" creature with "fiery eyes" was ready to emerge, New York would provide a welcome, and make Edgar and his "ungainly fowl" famous.

12 · The Raven *and the Peak of Tragedy*

THIS was to be known as "the house where *The Raven* was written." Since the days when he swam in the James River and tramped the nearby woods, he had always loved the countryside. Now, for a while at least, Edgar and Virginia and his aunt were to live in a farmhouse owned by Patrick Brennan. The farm occupied 216 acres adjacent to the Hudson, and high in the garret, where he and his young wife stayed, they could look down at the gleaming river and glimpse the green of the woods and meadows. Here, in his study, the inspiration that had been born when he first encountered poor Barnaby Rudge and his pet raven Grip was slowly taking shape. As he pondered over the poem, many strange images passed through his mind. Somehow, the bust of Pallas which stood on a shelf above the doorway seemed to be interwoven with these images.

The analytical faculty that he displayed in his stories controlled his thoughts. But his mind was a rare combination of theory and order balanced by unrestrained flights into fantasy. In creating his new poem, he would plan—but without rigidity. First must come the *single, unified impression or effect* that he advocated. It could not be *Truth,* "the satisfaction of the intellect," or *Passion,* "the excitement of the heart." These are best attained in prose, not poetry. Without question, *Beauty* is the "atmosphere and essence of the poem."

But a poem must have *tone.* What should be the *tone* of this poem? To Edgar, the answer was instantly apparent. No other tone was possible but that of *sadness.* "Melancholy is . . . the most legitimate of all the poetical tones."

What of the structure of the poem? To his mind came a device often used in poetry and song—the *refrain.* Repeated at the end of every stanza, the *refrain* is enjoyed by the reader or listener because of its repetition—and the sense of identity that it gives. The *refrain* is bound to make an impression; the audience learns it quickly because of "the force of monotone—both in sound and thought." Nevertheless, Edgar shook his head over it. The *refrain* is too simple—too primitive; it must be varied. The idea came to him. Of course! Use the monotone of sound—but vary the thought. And since the thought must be varied in the *refrain,* one further point was obvious: the *refrain* must be a *single word;* this would make it easier to vary the thought.

The analysis went on. He wanted a "non-reasoning" creature to repeat the *refrain* mechanically. The first thought, naturally, was of a parrot. But then *Barnaby Rudge's* croaking raven made a clamor in his mind. The black, ugly raven, the bird of ill-omen —this creature was far better than a parrot. The word he would repeat at the end of each stanza was "Nevermore!" and in a melancholy poem, what topic is the most melancholy of all? The answer sprang to his lips—*death!* All that remains to be answered is this question: *When is the topic of death most poetical?* Edgar gave the reply that he knew by heart; it came from the agony and fear that had grown inside him from the moment of his first tragedy:

When it most closely allies itself to *Beauty:* the death then of a beautiful woman is unquestionably the most poetical topic in the world, and equally is it beyond doubt that the lips best suited for such topic are those of a bereaved lover.

He pictured the setting, with the Raven entering the room and perching above his chamber door on the bust of Pallas. The lover, seated alone and dreaming of his "lost Lenore," at first asks the "ghastly grim and ancient Raven" a commonplace question: "Tell me what thy lordly name is . . ." The Raven answers, "Nevermore!" The lover believes he is merely hearing a bird "repeating a lesson learned by rote."

The plot of the poem became clearer to Edgar. As the Raven continues to answer with the same "Nevermore," the lover is excited by the repetition and the "melancholy character of the word itself," and asks questions of a different nature. Now they are personal, passionate ones of his lost love; and he asks them not because he *believes* the bird is a prophet, but because the *expected* "Nevermore" brings him a "frenzied pleasure," filling him with the "most delicious" and "most intolerable of sorrows."

Through this careful planning, the most important point became apparent to Edgar. The last question asked by the lover, and the Raven's final answer, are the *climax* of the poem. The effect here must be of "the utmost conceivable amount of sorrow and despair." To leave the lover in this most complete state of sorrow, it was necessary to think of the *last stanzas first*—to plan them *first*.

"Here then," said Edgar, "the poem may be said to have had its beginning, *at the end* where all works of art should begin. . . ."

Stanza by stanza, through the warm summer months and the fall of 1844, Edgar worked on *The Raven,* writing, polishing, and revising. It was to be the most perfectly planned and constructed poem ever created. The perfectionist poet weighed and tested each word, phrase and line, never satisfied—always changing, substituting, re-writing.

At the end of the year, *The Raven* was sold to the *American Whig Review,* but through special permission was first published in the *Evening Mirror* on January 29, 1845. In this issue, and in the *Weekly Mirror* of February 8th, Nathaniel Parker Willis prefaced the poem with a paragraph of praise seldom granted to an author.

In referring to "the following remarkable poem by Edgar Poe," he said,

In our opinion, it is the most effective single example of "fugitive poetry" ever published in this country; and unsurpassed in English poetry for subtle conception, masterly ingenuity of versification, and consistent, sustaining of imaginative lift and "pokerishness." It is one of these "dainties bred in a book" which we *feed* on. It will stick to the memory of *everybody* who reads it.

Beneath this paragraph appeared the title, *The Raven,* and the poem followed with its familiar opening stanza:

Once upon a midnight dreary, while I pondered weak and weary,
Over many a quaint and curious volume of forgotten lore,
While I nodded, nearly napping, suddenly there came a tapping,
As of someone gently rapping, rapping at my chamber door.
" 'Tis some visitor," I muttered, "tapping at my chamber door—
        Only this, and nothing more."

In the development of Edgar's plan, the student who had been poring over a volume and dreaming of his dead sweetheart watches the Raven flutter in and is amused by its actions and odd appearance. From a first question, which is asked in jest, the poem rises to a climax of self-torture and deep sorrow. The lover is painfully reminded of what he already knows—there is no hope of clasping a "rare and radiant maiden whom the angels name Lenore," and he shrieks,

"Leave my loneliness unbroken!—quit the bust above my door!
Take thy beak from out my heart, and take thy form from off my door!"

In the end, the Raven's shadow becomes the symbol of the permanency of the lover's sorrow:

And the lamp-light o'er him streaming throws his shadow on the floor;
And my soul from out that shadow that lies floating on the floor
        Shall be lifted—nevermore!

Late in 1844, Edgar accepted a regular position on the New York *Evening Mirror.* Little money had been coming in, and his Aunt Maria was worried. With the summer at an end they would have to leave the farm and move back to the city. On her own initiative, she had called upon Nathaniel Parker Willis, the *Mirror's* editor, to plead with him on Edgar's account. The position paid a small salary, but, as always, Edgar could not afford to be particular.

The year brought another of the tales of *ratiocination* and the return of the astute Monsieur Dupin. *The Purloined Letter* was published in the *Gift* for 1845. Again, Edgar shares the experience with Dupin, to whom the Prefect of the Parisian police appeals for help. The matter is a delicate one—"a certain document of the last importance has been purloined from the royal apartments." The document, an intimate letter, if disclosed to a third person, would involve the honor of a member of the royal household.

Dupin is not presented with his typical case of a complex murder where a scientific analysis of clues is needed. The one who has stolen the letter is known; he is a minister who obviously intends to blackmail the woman who had received it. For three months the French police, certain that the minister has the letter near at hand, have ransacked his apartment, searching in every nook and corner—but with no success. Dupin's assignment now is to find the letter.

In developing the character and superb ability of Dupin, Edgar chooses a light approach. Dupin advises the Prefect to make another thorough search of the minister's quarters. A month later he returns to see the detective and report that the letter has not been recovered. The Prefect offers a reward of 50,000 francs to anyone who can find it.

"In that case," replied Dupin, opening a drawer, and producing a check-book, "you may as well fill me up a check for the amount mentioned. When you have signed it, I will hand you the letter."

To the astonishment of his companion and the Prefect, he produces the letter from his writing desk and hands it to the waiting official. Dupin explains the reasoning that led him to the location of the letter. The crafty minister had expected that his rooms would be given a microscopic search. As a result, he had avoided "all the ordinary nooks of concealment." It had been placed, with a deliberately careless appearance, in an ordinary card-rack next to a half-dozen visiting cards. It seemed to be an old letter, soiled, crumpled, and torn almost in two. The police had never suspected that a letter so valuable would be left lying before them, with no attempt at concealment.

Upon leaving the Brennan farm, Edgar and his family moved to a rooming house at Number 15 Amity Street. In the literary world, Edgar resumed a friendly relationship with Rufus Griswold, the anthologist, with whom he had quarreled. Always a man with more than one iron in the fire, Edgar began contributing to a new periodical, *The Broadway Journal,* whose editor was Charles

Briggs. In February, 1845, Edgar left the *Mirror* to take an editorial position on the *Journal*.

In the passing months, Edgar, who had long been concerned with literary plagiarism, wrote a series of articles for the *Journal* in which he made serious accusations against Longfellow. These charges of plagiarism appeared to be unfounded, but Edgar had been carried away by the personal battle he had been waging against plagiarism, and, above all, by his anger at the lack of protection for American authors. International copyright laws did not exist, and unscrupulous American publishers could steal British novels and short stories at will. These could be reprinted without paying anything to the author, and, under these conditions, many publishers could see no reasons for purchasing works by American writers.

But beyond this, in his literary criticisms for magazines and newspapers, Edgar had acquired a reputation for being extremely severe. He had been especially sharp in his criticisms of the New England authors. Friends and discerning individuals who knew of his frustrations and continuing poverty understood that Edgar often lashed out at others in bitterness over the world's injustices. Longfellow refused to be drawn into a war of accusations with Edgar, and years later made a generous comment which illustrated that he was aware of Edgar's problems:

The harshness of his [Edgar's] criticisms I have never attributed to anything but the irritation of a sensitive nature, shaped by some indefinite sense of wrong.

The home situation, revolving around Virginia's health, seemed to be somewhat stable, for on May 4, 1845, when Edgar wrote to his friend Thomas, he spoke of the hours of work:

. . . The fact is, that being seized, of late, with a fit of industry, I put so many irons in the fire all at once, that I have been quite unable to get them out. For the last three or four months I have been working 14 or 15 hours a day—hard at it all the time—and so, whenever I took pen in hand to write, I found I was neglecting something that *would be* attended to. I never knew what it was to be a slave before.

But talent and hard work had not helped to supply his greatest need. "As yet, Thomas, I have made no money," he wrote. "I am as poor now as ever I was in my life—except in hope, which is by no means bankable. I have taken a 3d pecuniary interest in the 'Broadway Journal,' and for everything I have written for it have been, of course, so much out of pocket."

At the end of the letter, Edgar showed that he still possessed his sense of humor: " 'The Raven' has had a great 'run,' Thomas—but I wrote it for the express purpose of running—just as I did the 'Gold-Bug,' you know. The bird beat the bug, though, all hollow."

During the year 1845, Edgar, now reaping some of the benefits of his literary fame, began to widen his social life. He was accepted in literary circles and enjoyed attending affairs that were held at the homes of other writers or patrons of the arts. At these meetings Virginia was often seen with him.

He also began to develop a friendship with Mrs. Frances Sargent Osgood, whose poetry he had praised in one of his lectures. Mrs. Osgood later described her first meeting with Edgar at the Astor House, in March, 1845:

A few days previous, Mr. Willis had handed me, at the table d'hote, that strange and thrilling poem entitled "The Raven," saying that the author wanted my opinion of it. Its effect upon me was so singular, so like that of "weird, unearthly music," that it was with a feeling almost of dread, I heard he desired an introduction.

Mrs. Osgood described how he appeared to her at their first meeting:

With his proud and beautiful head erect, his dark eyes flashing with the electric light of feeling and of thought, a peculiar, an inimitable blending of sweetness and hauteur in his expression and manner, he greeted me, calmly, gravely, almost coldly; yet with so marked an earnestness that I could not help being deeply impressed by it. From that moment until his death we were friends . . .

Mrs. Osgood became a friend of the entire family and was often invited by Virginia to visit at the Poe house. She was the authoress of two volumes of poetry, and soon an unusual poetic "courtship" began between her and Edgar. They exchanged verses which were printed in the *Broadway Journal,* hers modestly titled *To* ————, and his replies headed, *To F*————. This close association was bound to cause some comment. Mrs. Osgood, a pretty woman of thirty-four, was the wife of the American painter, Samuel S. Osgood, who was later to paint a portrait of Edgar.

In her admiration for Virginia and her visits to the family, Mrs. Osgood seemed to offer evidence that friendship was her only motive and that she had no intention of conducting a secret romance with Edgar. Later she wrote with sincerity of the association:

Of the charming love and confidence that existed between his wife and himself, always delightfully apparent to me, in spite of the many little poetical episodes, in which the impassioned romance of his temperament impelled him to indulge; of this I cannot speak too earnestly—too warmly. I believe she was the only woman whom he ever truly loved.

As a mark of Edgar's increasing fame, the New York firm of Wiley and Putnam agreed to publish a collection of his tales. The volume was announced on July 19, 1845, but its contents proved disappointing to Edgar. It was a small edition of only twelve stories, including a number of the most popular ones. Later Edgar commented, "The collection of tales issued by W. & P. were selected by a gentleman whose taste does not coincide with my own, from 72 written by me at various times—and those chosen are *not* my best—nor do they fairly represent me—in any respect." The stories had been selected by Evert Duyckinck, an experienced editor, who was to become Edgar's friend and literary agent.

Encouraged by the steady sales of Edgar's stories, Wiley and Putnam next launched a volume of his poetry. Titled *The Raven and Other Poems,* the book was published in November, 1845. The collection of poems (which sold for thirty-one cents) included both the later and early ones. Among "Poems Written in Youth" were *Tamerlane, Al Aaraaf,* and *To Helen*. Again, in the Preface, Edgar made sharply critical remarks. But in his last statement there could be no question about his high ideals:

With me poetry has been not a purpose, but a passion; and the passions should be held in reverence; they must not—they cannot at will be excited with an eye to the paltry compensations, or the more paltry commendations, of mankind.

For allowing his "Poems Written in Youth" to be published, Edgar apologized, saying that "Private reasons . . . have induced me, after some hesitation, to republish these, the crude compositions of my earliest boyhood."

The volume of poetry was dedicated "To the Noblest of her Sex—Elizabeth Barrett Barrett" (Mrs. Browning). Earlier, in reviewing a collection of her poems for the *Broadway Journal,* Edgar had used ecstatic terms to paint her as "the greatest—the most glorious of her sex." Here he may have been combining his high opinion of her poems with the intense admiration he felt for women of creative ability. In the future, because he was drawn into new literary circles, he was to associate with other talented women. The exchange of ideas, as well as their attentions and flattery, was bound to stimulate him. The key to Edgar's interest in them can be found in the phrase that Mrs. Osgood used to describe him: "the impassioned romance of his temperament." *Beauty* had been almost an obsession with him ever since childhood: the beauty of words and of nature; the beauty of women; the constant search for ideal beauty; and now, to all these was added the beauty of the mind, of the intellect. These were the living forces that drove him on—that released the most fanciful imagination the world had ever known.

The ordinary events of life continued, with work on the *Broadway Journal,* and with the accustomed pattern of moving. The family had been living at Number 195 Broadway, a run-down house in a tenement district, but in mid-1845 they returned to Amity Street, taking lodgings at Number 85. Combined with the problem of poverty was Virginia's constant illness. On August 8, 1845, Edgar wrote to Neilson Poe, telling of conditions at home:

She [Virginia] has been, and is still, in precarious health. About four years ago she ruptured a blood-vessel, in singing, and has never recovered from the accident. I fear that she never will. Mrs. Clemm is quite well:—both beg to be kindly remembered.

Through the efforts of James Russell Lowell, Edgar was asked to give a lecture and read one of his poems before the Boston Lyceum. For some time preceding the scheduled date of October 16, 1845, Edgar had been in a nervous, depressed condition. He had promised to write a new poem for the occasion but was unable to do so.

The poem he finally chose to read was one of his earliest—*Al Aaraaf.* Because of its length and the difficulty of its hidden symbolism, the audience became bored and restless. Edgar then read *The Raven,* which he was asked to do at almost every public affair, and received enthusiastic applause. But Edgar was deeply disappointed, and in this state, which was aggravated by a sense of personal guilt, he once more turned to drink. He had suffered an unhappy experience with a lecture presented some months earlier at the New York Historical Society, on the topic of "The Poets and Poetry of America." Because of bad weather very few people attended; the lecture was canceled and the money returned. An office boy from the *Journal,* who attended the lecture, later wrote:

It was a little thing, it is true, but he was a man easily upset by little things. The next morning he came to the office, leaning on the arm of a friend, intoxicated with wine.

The failure of the Boston lecture found him even more disturbed. Both Boston and New York papers were very critical of his performance. Edgar was particularly angered over an insulting article by Cornelia M. Walter, editor of the *Boston Evening Transcript,* who commented, ". . . if he [Edgar] uttered poesy in the first instance, it was certainly of a most prosaic order," and "The audience now thinned so rapidly and made so much commotion in their departure that we lost the beauties of the composition. . . ."

Edgar permitted himself to be lured into a controversy in which he made sneering remarks about Bostonians:

. . . We were born there—and perhaps it is just as well not to mention that we are heartily ashamed of the fact. The Bostonians are very well in their way. Their hotels are bad. Their pumpkin pies are delicious. Their poetry is not so good. Their Common is no common thing—and the duck-pond might answer—if its answer could be heard for the frogs.

But with all these good qualities the Bostonians have no soul. They have always evinced towards us individually, the basest ingratitude for the services we rendered them in enlightening them about the originality of Mr. Longfellow. When we accepted, therefore, an invitation to "deliver" a poem in Boston—we accepted it simply and solely, because we had a curiosity to know how it felt to be publicly *hissed.* . . . The Bostonians are well-bred—as *very* dull persons very generally are.

As for Miss Walter, Edgar said, "The adorable creature has been telling a parcel of fibs about us, by way of revenge for something that we did to Mr. Longfellow (who admires her very much) and for calling her 'a pretty little witch' into the bargain."

His never-ending desire to be in complete charge of a periodical led him to make arrangements for the purchase of the *Broadway Journal.* He had got into a disagreement with Charles Briggs, who soon withdrew from the publication. Later, Edgar bought out the interest of the third partner, John Bisco, and agreed to be fully responsible for the *Journal* and its debts. The deal was unfortunate. His anxiety to have a publication of his own had caused him to enter the world of practical business affairs—a world of which he had little knowledge. What followed was a period of desperate borrowing. Horace Greeley endorsed a personal note for $50, needed to pay Bisco. Other authors, including Thomas Holley

Chivers and Fitz-Greene Halleck, were appealed to, but whatever money Edgar received was not sufficient. In Edgar's opinion, a sum of about $140 would have saved the *Broadway Journal,* but there was no way of obtaining it. Edgar sold a half-interest in the *Journal* to Thomas H. Lane; he was willing to sacrifice his ownership in the hope that the publication would continue. As in previous cases of tension and financial problems, Edgar entered a period of severe mental depression. In November, 1845, he wrote to his agent, Evert Duyckinck,

For the first time during two months I find myself entirely myself— dreadfully sick and depressed, but still myself. I seem to have just awakened from some horrible dream, in which all was confusion, and suffering. . . . I really believe that I have been mad—but indeed I have had abundant reason to be so.

On January 3, 1846, Edgar announced that the *Broadway Journal* was ceasing publication. "I now, as its Editor," he said, "bid farewell—as cordially to foes as to friends."

Only a month earlier, one of his most sensational stories, *The Facts of M. Valdemar's Case,* had appeared in the *American Review.* Its basis was the strong interest Edgar had shown in mesmerism. In August, 1844, the *Columbian Magazine* had printed his *Mesmeric Revelation,* in which Edgar played the role of the mesmerist in placing his patient, Mr. Vankirk, into a hypnotic trance. Vankirk was in an advanced state of consumption, the same disease that had destroyed Virginia's health. In the story Vankirk's statements explain why he has sent for the mesmerist: "I need not tell you how skeptical I have hitherto been on the topic of the soul's immortality." The conclusion of his long explanation is that he wishes Edgar to mesmerize him and then pose a series of questions about immortality, with some hope that in this strange hypnotic world Vankirk might find the *truth* concerning immortality. Whatever was discovered in the "sleep-waking" state bordering upon death is never revealed. Edgar becomes alarmed at Vankirk's condition and awakes him from the trance. The man dies and his corpse has the "stern rigidity of stone," indicating that he *had been dead* for some time. During the last part of the questioning, was he speaking to Edgar "from out the regions of the shadows"? No answer is offered.

Continuing his fascination with mesmerism, Edgar turned, two years later, to *M. Valdemar's Case,* writing an incredible tale of a dying man who is placed in a hypnotic trance. A series of questions to M. Valdemar reveal that he has no pain and that he is close to death. When he is next asked if he has been sleeping, Valdemar replies, "Yes;—no;—I *have been* sleeping—and now—now—*I am dead.*"

To Edgar, "It was evident that, so far, death (or what is usually termed death) had been arrested by the mesmeric process." The astounding account continues with M. Valdemar remaining in his sleep-waking state for *"an interval of nearly seven months."*

The last part of the story achieves a gruesome, revolting effect. When Valdemar is asked to explain his feelings or wishes, he screams hideously, "For God's sake!—quick!—quick!—put me to sleep—or, quick!—waken me!—quick!—*I say to you that I am dead!*"

He is brought out of his mesmeric trance, and then: "his whole frame at once—within the space of a single minute, or even less, shrunk—crumbled, absolutely *rotted* away beneath my hands. Upon the bed, before the whole company, there lay a nearly liquid mass of loathsome—of detestable putrescence."

The scientific approach and the convincing realism of the style and details made many readers believe that Edgar was reporting a factual case. In 1846, Londoners read, gasped, and accepted as true fact the reprinted, threepenny pamphlet entitled, *Mesmerism, In Articulo Mortis. An Astounding and Horrifying Narrative. Shewing the Extraordinary Power of Mesmerism in Arresting the Progress of Death.* By Edgar A. Poe, Esq. of New York.

As 1846 opened, Edgar was once again without employment. While he had always been able to draw upon a reserve strength to fight against poverty and discouragement, there was now evidence that he was breaking down. For a period of four months, from February to July, he was too ill to write. Fortunately, for the summer months, the family was able to move to a farmhouse at Fordham, thirteen miles from New York. Here, in the midst of the countryside that Edgar loved, they lived in a small cottage at the top of a hill. Edgar tried to rest and recuperate, but circumstances could not allow him complete ease. Virginia's health had grown steadily worse. Mrs. Mary Gove, a visitor at the Fordham cottage, described what she had observed:

. . . Mrs. Poe looked very young; she had large black eyes, and a pearly whiteness of complexion, which was a perfect pallor. Her pale face, her brilliant eyes, and her raven hair gave her an unearthly look.

One felt that she was almost a disrobed spirit, and when she coughed it was made certain that she was rapidly passing away.

Edgar's creative powers were on the decline and the year 1846 was to be one of lesser accomplishment. He had turned to writing literary criticisms for *Godey's Lady's Book,* but in May, 1846, *Godey's* published the first installment of *The Literati of New York,* a series which ran from May through October and offered Edgar's personal criticisms of thirty-eight authors. His comments, often severe, brought protests from annoyed writers and their friends. Actually, Edgar was revealing his judgment of the contemporary authors as sincerely as he could, or, as he described the *Literati,* "Some Honest Opinions at Random Respecting their Autorial Merits, with Occasional Words of personality."

On later reflection, he realized that he had made mistakes. A letter to George W. Eveleth contained an apologetic explanation:

You will see that I have discontinued *The Literati* in Godey's Mag. I was forced to do so, because I found that people insisted on considering them elaborate criticisms when I had no other design than critical gossip. . . .

Do not trust, in making up your library, to the "opinions" in the Godey series. I *meant* "honest"—but my meaning is not as fully made out as I could wish. I thought too little of the series myself to guard sufficiently against haste, inaccuracy, or prejudice.

He was even in a mood to refer good-humoredly to his antagonisms toward Bostonians—especially those uncultured members of the "frog-pond" who, according to Edgar, croaked loudly to conceal their ignorance: "The Frogpondians have badgered me so much that I fear I am apt to fall into prejudices about them."

The entire year was not devoted to literary criticisms, for in November, 1846, one of his most powerful stories, *The Cask of Amontillado,* was printed in *Godey's.* The theme is stated in the opening sentence: "The thousand injuries of Fortunato I had borne as I best could, but when he ventured upon insult, I vowed revenge."

In other stories Edgar, as the main character, has committed sadistic acts and savage murders. In *The Tell-Tale Heart* the old man with the "vulture eye" is killed; and in *The Black Cat,* a fit of rage drives a madman to murder his wife. In these tales, conscience and psychological torment play an important part, and there is retribution at the end. But in *The Cask of Amontillado,* the enemy who has a weakness for Amontillado wine is lured to the damp, cavernous vaults and coaxed into a state of intoxication. He is chained in a cell-like recess, a niche, and his murderer walls in the entrance with building stone and mortar. Fortunato is buried alive. It is a story of fierce revenge and of a murderer without conscience. The guilty man is never punished. At the story's end Edgar writes,

I forced the last stone into its position; I plastered it up. Against the new masonry I re-erected the old rampart of bones. For the half of a century no mortal has disturbed them. *In pace requiescat!*

For Edgar, the world of reality in the year 1846 had been a painful one. He had reached the height of his career; his works were published world-wide, and his name was mentioned with admiration in literary circles everywhere. His two creations, *The Raven* and *The Gold Bug,* had achieved a popularity never equaled by any other works. Yet his years of feverish labor had resulted only in poverty and broken health.

But the year 1847 opened with tragic promise. Virginia was dying—fading away in the final stages of consumption. In her five-year struggle she had been near death a number of times, had rallied and regained her strength. Now, seated at her bedside, Edgar waited numbly, all hope gone. Mrs. Mary Gove had come to the cottage to offer her help. She was appalled by the conditions she saw:

. . . There was no clothing on the bed, which was only straw, but a snow white spread and sheets. The weather was cold, and the sick lady had the dreadful chills that accompany the hectic fever of consumption. She lay on the straw bed, wrapped in her husband's great-coat, with a large tortoise-shell cat on her bosom. The wonderful cat (Caterina) seemed conscious of her great usefulness. The coat and the cat were the sufferer's only means of warmth, except as her husband held her hands, and her mother her feet.

Mrs. Gove summoned Mrs. Marie Louise Shew, a nurse, and the two joined efforts to provide the comforts Virginia desperately needed, including a featherbed and warm bed-clothing. Mrs. Shew, who was to be of great help to Edgar later, went about soliciting money for the family and was able to collect sixty dollars. Virginia lingered on, fighting painfully for breath. Hours before her death she took the picture that she had kept near her, beneath the pillow, and placed it in Mrs. Shew's hands. It was a picture of Edgar.

Virginia also gave Mrs. Shew a small jewel case that had belonged to his mother.

On January 30, 1847, Virginia died. She was taken to the burial vault of the Valentine family, the owners of the Fordham cottage. Years later, her remains were taken to Baltimore and given a final resting place next to her husband's grave.

She was twenty-four years old, and by a curious coincidence she died at the same age that Edgar's mother and brother Henry had died. Almost a year before her death, on St. Valentine's Day of 1846, Virginia had composed a simple poem of her own as a valentine for the man she had always worshiped. In its yearning for a peace and security that she had never known, and in her deep faith and love, her willingness to endure poverty and suffering with her beloved Eddy, and her hope for the future, it presented a touching illustration of Virginia's character. She had arranged the first letters of the lines to spell her husband's name:

> Ever with thee I wish to roam—
> Dearest my life is thine.
> Give me a cottage for my home
> And a rich old cypress vine,
> Removed from the world with its sin and care
> And the tattling of many tongues.
> Love alone shall guide us when we are there—
> Love shall heal my weakened lungs;
> And Oh, the tranquil hours we'll spend,
> Never wishing that others may see!
> Perfect ease we'll enjoy, without thinking to lend
> Ourselves to the world and its glee—
> Ever peaceful and blissful we'll be.

13 · *The Last Outpouring*

THE shock of Virginia's death, following upon the months of his own mental depression and illness, brought Edgar to a complete breakdown. He was now a patient who had to be nursed by Mrs. Clemm and Mrs. Shew. The daughter of a doctor, Mrs. Shew showed an unusual understanding of Edgar's condition and made her own diagnosis. She reported her findings to the physician, Dr. Valentine Mott:

. . . when Mr. Poe was well, his pulse beat only ten regular beats, after which it suspended, or intermitted (as doctors say). I decided that in his best health he had lesion of one side of the brain, and as he could not bear stimulants or tonics, without producing insanity, I did not feel much hope that he could be raised up from brain fever brought on by extreme suffering of mind and body. . . .

In his brain fever Edgar babbled to her of the past. His main worry was that he would be unable to keep his promises to the publishers, and he begged Mrs. Shew to copy the stories he would dictate. He had a strange fear that if he failed in his obligations to the publishers they would "revenge themselves by saying all sorts of evil of him if he should die."

But Edgar still had the fierce urge to live and to create. This powerful will helped him recover from his mental and physical collapse. While he delved in his imagination for new ideas, an older composition, the review of Nathaniel Hawthorne's *Twice Told Tales,* appeared in *Godey's Lady's Book* for November, 1847.

In spite of his anguish, his creativeness could not be suppressed, and in the fall of 1847 he completed one of his most exquisite poems, *Ulalume.* The poem was inevitably centered about Virginia and the deep, spiritual nature of their love which would still guide his actions. Perhaps he was fortunate in being able to release his grief and pain through poetic expression. In *Ulalume* the familiar touches are there—the ever-present atmosphere of death and the tragic loss of a loved one. At the end, the lover who may be tempted to turn to new loves is reminded, at the vault of his "lost Ulalume" of the unchanging bond that still exists:

> Then my heart it grew ashen and sober
> As the leaves that were crisped and sere—
> As the leaves that were withering and sere;
> And I cried—"It was surely October
>   On *this* very night of last year
>   That I journeyed—I journeyed down here—
>   That I brought a dread burden down here!
>   On this night of all nights in the year,
>   Ah, what demon has tempted me here?
> Well I know, now, this dim lake of Auber—
>   This misty mid region of Weir—

> Well I know, now, this dark tarn of Auber,
> This ghoul-haunted woodland of Weir."

With his return to health, Edgar again dreamed of his own magazine. On January 4, 1848, he wrote to George Eveleth: "I am resolved to be my own publisher. To be controlled is to be ruined. My ambition is great. If I succeed, I put myself (within 2 years) in possession of a fortune and infinitely more." He spoke of plans to travel through the South and the West in search of subscribers.

During this same period, his brilliant mind was concerned with the most ambitious work he had ever attempted. On February 3, 1848, he gave a lengthy lecture on his forthcoming prose poem *Eureka,* described, in its printed form, as "An Essay on the Material and Spiritual Universe." The subject matter was so complex that much of it left the audience in a baffled state. But it seems clear that in *Eureka,* while he was often obscure and disorganized, his theories were related to scientific findings that came years later.

Eureka was written in prose form, but in the Preface Edgar wrote, "Nevertheless, it is as a Poem only that I wish this work to be judged after I am dead." He offered a summary of his theme; its scope was staggering:

> I design to speak *of the Physical, Metaphysical, and Mathematical— of the Material and Spiritual Universe; of its Essence, its Origin, its Creation, its present Condition and its Destiny.*

Eureka was a remarkable attempt to explain the laws and unity of the universe. In his unparalleled genius, Edgar had done what no other writer would have considered doing: he had turned from his astonishing successes in poetry, the short story, and literary criticism to an exploration of physics, offering a set of theories of extreme complexity.

In a letter to George Eveleth dated January 4, 1848, Edgar revealed how intensely he had suffered during Virginia's illness. A question had been brought up about the "irregularities" of his conduct. Edgar bared his soul to write an agonized account of the continual crisis and how it had affected him:

> Six years ago, a wife, whom I loved as no man ever loved before, ruptured a blood-vessel in singing. Her life was despaired of. I took leave of her forever & underwent all the agonies of her death. She recovered partially and I again hoped. At the end of a year the vessel broke again—I went through precisely the same scene. Again in about a year afterward. Then again—again—again & even once again at

varying intervals. Each time I felt all the agonies of her death—and at each accession of the disorder I loved her more dearly & clung to her life with more desperate pertinacity.

The hopeless existence led to a terrible change in him:

But I am constitutionally sensitive—nervous in a very unusual degree. I became insane, with long periods of horrible sanity. During these fits of absolute unconsciousness I drank, God only knows how often or how much. As a matter of course, my enemies referred the insanity to the drink rather than the drink to the insanity.

Edgar explained that after he had "nearly abandoned all hope of a permanent cure," he found one in the *death* of Virginia. Now he can endure her death "as becomes a man." But if the "oscillation" between hope and despair had continued, he would have lost his mind. "In the death of what was my life," he said, "then, I receive a new but—oh God! how melancholy an existence."

With *Eureka* scheduled for publication in June by George Putnam, Edgar embarked upon his tour of the South to seek subscribers for his *Stylus*. Some time in July, 1848, he returned to his native city of Richmond. Perhaps the anguished memories of the past, and of what might have been, overcame him, for once again he turned to drink for escape. John R. Thompson, the editor of the *Southern Literary Messenger,* wrote of the distressing situation:

. . . He remained here about 3 weeks, horribly drunk and discoursing "Eureka" every night to the audiences of the Bar Rooms. His friends tried to get him sober and set him to work but to no effect and were compelled at last to reship him to New York. I was very anxious for him to write something for me, while he remained here, but his lucid intervals were so brief and infrequent that it was quite impossible.

Thompson added that the *Messenger* had taken Edgar's essay, *The Rationale of Verse,* "more as an act of charity than anything else." He classed it as being "too bizarre and too technical for the general reader."

With the kindly Mrs. Marie Shew, who had come to the aid of the dying Virginia and then nursed Edgar through his illness, he developed a close friendship. One day during the summer of 1848 he came to her home at Number 51 Tenth Street in New York. Since his wife's death he had turned to her often for sympathy and advice. Now, with her encouragement, he sat down in a creative mood. He thought at first of writing a poem, but the sound of the bells from Grace Church interrupted his thoughts. He put down his pen and said, "It's no use. The bells are too noisy. I won't be able to write today."

Mrs. Shew smiled at him, and taking the pen, she wrote on the paper, "The Bells, by E. A. Poe," and beneath it "The little silver bells."

Edgar stared at the paper and then straightened up. A gleam of interest came into his eyes. He began to write quickly and soon finished the first stanza. He leaned back and pressed his hands to his face. "I can't do any more," he said. "I'm too tired."

"Try one more stanza," Mrs. Shew said. She thought for a moment. "Write about the heavy iron bells."

The idea appeared to inspire him, for he turned again to the poem. Minutes later he had written the second stanza. His energies then seemed completely exhausted and he was unable to continue.

The Bells, as with most of Edgar's works, was to have a number of revisions. He was a perfectionist who could not quit one of his creations until he believed that further improvement was impossible. John Sartain received the poem in its first form late in the year. He reported that it consisted of only eighteen lines. Edgar altered and enlarged it, and in November, 1849, *The Bells* in its final form was published in *Sartain's Union Magazine.*

The poem is remarkable, first of all, for its melodious sounds, created by combinations of vowels, and for its perfect rhythm and rhyme. But the skillful arrangement of the order of the bells, rising to a solemn climax, offers another example of Edgar's greatness. The poem begins in a mood of gayety:

> Hear the sledges with the bells—
>   Silver bells!
> What a world of merriment their melody foretells!

In the second stanza the happiness continues:

> Hear the mellow wedding bells,
>   Golden bells!

But soon we enter into a new mood with the "loud alarum bells—Brazen bells!" Edgar has created the terror of fire, the screams and shrieks "in the startled ear of night." Then from the "clamorous appealing" of the alarum bells we move to the finality:

> Hear the tolling of the bells—
>   Iron bells!
> What a world of solemn thought their monody compels!

The poem rises in a climax of despair, with the King of the Ghouls tolling the bells; and all now is sobbing, moaning, and groaning. Edgar may have been picturing life as he had experienced it—from the short moments of young happiness, to the fleeting rapture of marriage, through anguish, to the complete tragedy of death, where "on the human heart a stone" is rolled.

His association with Mrs. Shew, as with Mrs. Frances Osgood, was part of his need for a woman's care and understanding. But, in both cases, because of his search for affection and his uncontrollably romantic temperament, complications were bound to develop. Mrs. Osgood, made uncomfortable by the gossip that was linking Edgar's name with hers, contrived to change their close friendship into a casual one. Mrs. Shew faced the same situation and was driven to sending a firm letter to Edgar, saying that they must stop seeing each other. In the short remaining months of his life, he was to continue his quest for the ideal woman and for his concept of romantic love.

On June 10, 1848, Edgar was present at Lowell, Massachusetts, to deliver a lecture on "The Poets and Poetry of America." Here he met Mrs. Nancy Richmond, who in succeeding months was to become his dream woman—his "Annie." She was married to Charles Richmond, and appeared to lead a normal family life with her child, Caddy, and her younger sister, Sarah Heywood. Edgar made several visits to Lowell to lecture, and on these occasions he stayed at the Richmond home. It was evident that he had developed a strong affection for Mrs. Richmond, which she did not discourage.

His feelings for Annie, as with the other women he had idealized, were soon expressed in writing. In his tale *Landor's Cottage,* he gives a romantic picture of his first glimpse of her and the effect it made upon him. He describes approaching the cottage and rapping at the door:

Instantly a figure advanced to the threshold—that of a young woman about twenty-eight years of age—slender, or rather slight, and somewhat above the medium height.

On first glance Edgar was convinced he had found "the perfection of natural, in contradistinction from artificial *grace.*" His second impression was that of her *enthusiasm.* He went on to offer his explanation of womanly attraction:

So intense an expression of *romance,* perhaps I should call it, or of unworldliness, as that which gleamed from her deep-set eyes, had never so sunk into my heart of hearts before. I know not how it is, but this peculiar expression of the eye, wreathing itself occasionally into the lips, is the most powerful, if not absolutely the *sole* spell, which rivets my interest in woman.

The spell which a lovely woman could cast over him at a *first* meeting was an indication of his impulsive nature, his susceptibility to beauty, and, of course, his state of loneliness and self-pity. In *Landor's Cottage* he writes, "—'romance' and 'womanliness' seem to me convertible terms: and, after all, what man truly *loves* in woman is simply her *womanhood*." This provides another key to Edgar's romantic attitudes. In the future his love would not be for *a woman*, but for *womanhood*—the idea and the ideal.

During the same period, he began a close friendship with Mrs. Sarah Helen Whitman, a widow who had made an impression on him when he first saw her in Providence in 1845. She was another of the creative, intellectual women whom Edgar found attractive; her poetry had been published in many magazines. The difference in their age—she was forty-five, six years older than he—was of little matter to him; but she showed a constant awareness of it.

Mrs. Whitman had first seen Edgar at the home of Miss Anne Lynch, a society hostess who held many affairs for the "literati" of New York. At these, Edgar was noted as being "delighted in the society of superior women." Later, at Miss Lynch's suggestion, Mrs. Whitman sent a valentine to one of the parties where it was read to the guests. It was dedicated to Edgar and titled *The Raven*. In the poem Mrs. Whitman took a romantic view of the "grim and ancient Raven":

> Romeo talks of "White doves trooping,
> Amid crows athwart the night,"
> But to see thy dark wing swooping
> Down the silvery path of light,
> Amid swans and dovelets stooping,
> Were to me, a nobler sight. . . .

Edgar, although not present at the reading, heard of it and received a copy from Miss Lynch. The coincidence of Mrs. Whitman's name being "Helen" was bound to affect him sentimentally. He sent Mrs. Whitman a copy of the poem *To Helen* that he had written in 1831. But in her honor he composed a new poem with the same title, mailed it to her, and arranged for its publication in the *Union Magazine* of November, 1848.

By this time, Edgar's romantic interest was aroused and he

traveled to Providence to visit her. His highly emotional nature, and his tendency to be swept away by first romantic impulses, offer an explanation of his astonishing behavior. He told his "Helen" that he loved her, and, in the short time that they were together, he asked her to marry him. Upon leaving Mrs. Whitman he wrote a letter which again illustrates an over-emotional state:

. . . As you entered the room, pale, timid, hesitating, and evidently oppressed at heart; as your eyes rested appealingly, for one brief moment, upon mine, I felt, for the first time in my life, and tremblingly acknowledged, the existence of spiritual influences altogether out of the reach of the reason. I saw that you were *Helen—my* Helen—the Helen of a thousand dreams—she whose visionary lips had so often lingered upon my own in the divine trance of passion. . . .

While flattered by his attentions and attracted by him personally, Mrs. Whitman had no intention of being swept off her feet. She wrote to him, "Had I youth and health and beauty I would live for you and die with you. Now were I to allow myself to love you, I could only enjoy a bright brief hour of rapture and die." Further correspondence revealed that she was suffering from a nervous disorder.

Edgar's wooing continued during the month of October, but with no success. Mrs. Whitman made it plain that she had heard of his dissipations, and of the report that he had "great intellectual power, but no principle—no moral sense."

Upset by the accusation, Edgar wrote to "swear" that his soul was "incapable of dishonor," and that he had indulged only in "occasional follies and excesses." In the following weeks he seemed to have been in a dazed condition, not responsible for his actions. A scheduled lecture at Lowell was canceled after his arrival, but he spent some time with Annie Richmond. There he received a letter from Mrs. Whitman in which she still refused to answer "yes" to his marriage plea. This increased his mental disturbance and his depression drove him to a desperate act.

Arriving in Providence, he purchased two ounces of laudanum. He contemplated suicide, but, apparently unable to make the decision, traveled to Boston. There he wrote a letter to Annie Richmond, and followed it with another letter describing his attempt at suicide:

. . . I told you how my struggles were more than I could bear. I then reminded you of that holy promise which was the last I exacted from you in parting—that promise that under all circumstances, you would come to me on my bed of death. I implored you to come *then,* mentioning the place where I should be found in Boston. Having written this letter, I swallowed about half the laudanum, and hurried to the Post Office, *intending not to take the rest until I saw you* . . .

He explained that before he reached the Post Office his "reason was entirely gone" and he never mailed the letter. Fortunately, the large dose of laudanum would not stay down; it was "rejected" from his stomach, and afterward he became very ill. A friend took care of him, and some time later he returned to Providence. The unreliability of his actions is evident in the visit to Annie Richmond and his imploring letter to her—both timed, inconsistently, with his marriage proposal to Helen Whitman. This type of erratic pattern in his affairs with women would continue in the future.

In November, 1848, in spite of the objections of her mother, Mrs. Whitman agreed to marry Edgar on condition that he promise to stop all drinking. He gave her the promise and returned to his home at Fordham, where his aunt welcomed him back. Within the next month a series of confused incidents occurred which resulted in a complete separation of the pair. Mrs. Whitman, in her explanation, stressed that the engagement was a *conditional* one, not only in respect to Edgar's drinking habits, but also in the agreement that her mother's permission must be given. Her mother consented reluctantly on December 22nd, and Edgar set the date for the wedding, presumably on the following Monday. Then Mrs. Whitman received a letter cautioning her "against this imprudent marriage" and informing her that Edgar had broken his promise.

Although he denied it, the evidence seemed to her beyond dispute. She and her mother agreed that the wedding must be canceled and that Edgar should return to New York. Additional facts seem to indicate that both Edgar and Mrs. Whitman, after calm discussion with friends, may have realized that the marriage plans were too hasty. Whether accurate or not, Mrs. Whitman stated that, after her mother had insisted upon "the immediate termination of the interview, Mr. Poe then started up and left the house with an expression of bitter resentment at what he termed the 'intolerable insults' of my family. I never saw him more."

That Edgar had not been deeply wounded by the cancellation of the marriage to his "Helen," and the complete break that followed, is demonstrated in the letters he now wrote to Annie, his "pure, beautiful angel," the "wife" of his soul. In another letter he concluded,

But of one thing rest assured, "Annie"—from this day forth I shun the pestilential society of *literary women*. They are a heartless, unnatural, venomous, dishonorable *set* with no guiding principle but inordinate self-esteem. Mrs. Osgood is the *only* exception I know . . .

Now, as though fate had ordered that he be given one last chance to release the remaining fragments of his creative genius, Edgar turned again to writing feverishly. An incident that had appeared in the *Broadway Journal* in 1845 came to his mind. He recalled his readings of the *Chronicles,* by Jean Froissart, a medieval historian and poet, containing an account of a happening so horrible that it could not be forgotten. During court festivities, Charles VI of France and five of his nobles decide to costume themselves as satyrs. They cover their clothing with pitch and flax. In the midst of the merrymaking, the flammable pitch catches fire. The five nobles, linked together by chains, are burned to death. Charles is free, and dives into the water to save his life.

Edgar's astonishing memory had stored the incident until it could be used. Now his imagination dictated a new, startling twist to the plot. Why should the burning be accidental, he asked himself? Why not a terrible revenge? The grim prospect pleased him. Hop-Frog, a crippled dwarf, was the court jester, serving a cruel king. Whenever a masquerade was held at court, the king would call upon Hop-Frog and the beautiful girl Trippetta to suggest characters and arrange costumes. Edgar now saw the remaining incidents of the plot.

Both Hop-Frog and Trippetta are summoned to the presence of the king and his seven cabinet members. Hop-Frog, who hates wine, is forced to drink, and when Trippetta protests, a goblet of wine is thrown in her face. Threatened by the king, and ordered to think of something to break the "everlasting sameness," Hop-Frog suggests that the monarch and his ministers costume themselves as ourang-outangs, covering their garments with tar and flax. In the end, Hop-Frog achieves his gruesome revenge, and after announcing, "this is my last jest," he disappears with his friend, Trippetta.

In writing to Annie about *Hop-Frog,* Edgar offered some interesting information:

. . . The 5 prose pages I finished yesterday are called—what do you think?—I am sure you will never guess—*Hop-Frog!* Only think of *your*

Eddy writing a story with *such* a name as "Hop-Frog"! You would never guess the subject (which is a terrible one) from the title, I am sure. It will be published in a weekly paper, of Boston, called "The Flag of Our Union"—not a *very* respectable journal, perhaps, in a literary point of view, but one that pays as high prices as most of the Magazines.

The prices mentioned were five dollars for a "Graham page," and the same amount for a sonnet.

In turning to the field of science-fantasy for *Mellonta Tauta,* Edgar allowed his imagination to run free in an area that had always fascinated him—the world of the future. *Mellonta Tauta* (Greek for "Things of the Future") appeared in *Godey's Lady's Book* in February, 1849, with the heading ON BOARD BALLOON "SKYLARK," APRIL 1, 2848. Edgar had chosen April Fool's Day to offer some of his prophecies, to repeat theories from *Eureka,* and, in the course of a balloon voyage, to satirize the customs and actions of his own world.

Once more Edgar was to move from the field of prose and scientific imagination to one of the highest and purest imagination—his greatest love, poetry. In the spring of 1849 he was at work polishing a poem that he had recited in public as early as 1845. His sister Rosalie recalled hearing it again, a year later. In its final form there was no question that *Annabel Lee* was inspired by his wife, Virginia. Mrs. Osgood had said, "I believe she was the only woman he ever truly loved." Whatever happened in the agonizing months after Virginia's death, the lonely man looking for forgetfulness, the search for understanding and affection—these weighed little when placed alongside the deep, unchanging love he had shown through the years for the little cousin who became his wife. He married her over all objections, and in *Annabel Lee* wrote:

> But our love it was stronger by far than the love
> Of those who were older than we—
> Of many far wiser than we—
> And neither the angels in heaven above,
> Nor the demons down under the sea,
> Can ever dissever my soul from the soul
> Of the beautiful Annabel Lee.

Early in 1849, Edgar received a letter from Edward Patterson, editor of *The Spectator,* a weekly newspaper published in Oquawka, Illinois. Patterson showed some interest in Edgar's dream project —*The Stylus.* Edgar answered with enthusiasm, stating that "Experience, not less than the most mature reflection on this topic, assured me that no *cheap* magazine can ever again prosper *in America.*" His goal was to aim high, "address the intellect," and publish a magazine that would sell for five dollars a year. Edgar's plan was to make an extensive tour through the West and the South in a search for subscribers.

To Edgar's delight, Patterson replied with a generous offer:

I will furnish an office and take upon myself the sole charge and expense of Publishing a Magazine (name to be suggested by you) to be issued in monthly numbers at Oquawka, Illinois . . . at the rate of $5 per annum.

Patterson promised Edgar the "entire editorial control." Edgar quickly responded that he was starting for Richmond, that Patterson should write to him there, and went on to state ". . . I am not overstocked with money (what poor devil author is?)" The inevitable request for an advance followed—this time for fifty dollars.

Patterson sent the money and events began to move rapidly. The cottage at Fordham, a place of painful memories, was to be closed, and Aunt Maria would stay with Estelle Lewis, a family friend, whose poetry Edgar had edited. The farewell scene between Edgar and his aunt was one of touching sadness. Was it possible that the suffering and the misfortune of their years together led them to expect only the worst? Or was it more than that—a presentiment, or a sensing of the inevitable tragedy that was in the air? Edgar tried to offer hope to the woman who had been both his aunt and his mother.

"God bless you, my own darling mother," he said. "Do not fear for Eddy! See how good I will be while I am away from you, and will come back to love and comfort you."

On this June 30th, 1849, the weather was bright and sunny, but aboard the steamboat the two seemed to be enveloped in the shadows. They kissed goodbye, and she turned away to walk to the docks, where she stood waving at him. Her entire life had been one of sacrifice, and in the past eighteen years of devotion to "Eddy" she had believed in him with a simple, unchanging faith. Her "Eddy" had become famous, but, except for brief glimpses of happiness, the years had brought her only poverty and suffering. Fame had meant little in the way of comfort and ease for Aunt Maria; but she did not mind.

She watched the steamboat move away from the docks, her eyes fastened to his figure until nothing but a blur remained. He would never return.

Edgar arrived in Philadelphia early in July and stopped to visit John Sartain, editor of the *Union Magazine*. The events that followed cannot be pieced together accurately. That Edgar was either drinking or ill appears certain. He is reported to have told Sartain of several unbelievable occurrences: the first was that two men he had met on the New York train were plotting to kill him. He then said that he had been in Philadelphia's Moyamensing Prison because of a suspicion that he had been trying to pass a fifty-dollar counterfeit note.

He seemed to have had a strange dream or vision that he was ill with cholera. This was probably caused by his fear of the cholera epidemic that was prevalent in Philadelphia at the time. On July 7th, he wrote the first of a series of wild, incoherent letters to his aunt:

I have been *so* ill—have had the cholera, or spasms quite as bad, and can now hardly hold the pen.

The very instant you get this, *come* to me. The joy of seeing you will almost compensate for our sorrows. We can but die together. It is no use to reason with *me* now; I must die. . . .

I was never *really* insane, except on occasions where my heart was touched.

I have been taken to prison once since I came here for getting drunk; but *then* I was not. It was about Virginia.

At home, his aunt had meanwhile become alarmed at not hearing from him. On July 9th, she wrote to Mrs. Richmond: "Eddy has been gone ten days, and I have not heard one word from him. Do you wonder that I *am* distracted? I fear everything. . . ."

Edgar arrived in Richmond on July 14th. He had written another letter to his aunt, and now, in a third one, his mental disturbance was still apparent: "I got here with two dollars over—of which I enclose you one. Oh God, my Mother, shall we ever again meet? If possible, oh COME! . . ."

But, a week later, his condition appeared to be better. He began visiting his old friends in Richmond, and set to work on the promotion plans for his *Stylus*. On August 17, 1849, he lectured on "The Poetic Principle" to a large crowd.

The return to Richmond must have brought with it the pain of old memories. Perhaps he walked by John Allan's home to gaze at its familiar outlines and lose himself in the echoes of the past. Neither his Aunt Nancy nor Mrs. Allan was in town. But he did stop in to visit and chat with his childhood sweetheart, Catherine Poitiaux.

Naturally, his thoughts turned to the one who had been his first love, Elmira Shelton. Her husband had died, so Edgar now felt free to call upon her. After a first meeting, he attempted to renew their old romance. Elmira described what happened:

. . . when he did call again he renewed his addresses. I laughed at it; he looked very serious and said he was in earnest and had been thinking about it for a long time. Then I found out that he was very serious and I became serious. I told him if he would not take a positive denial he must give me time to consider of it. . . .

Before he left, Edgar spoke of a presentiment that he would never see her any more. Whether Elmira agreed to marry him or not, has never been determined. She said, "I was not engaged to Poe when he left here, but there was a partial understanding, but I do not think I should have married him under any circumstances." But in a letter to Maria Clemm on September 22, 1849, she appeared to indicate that she had accepted Edgar's proposal.

In Norfolk, where he lectured once more on the topic of "The Poetic Principle," Susan Ingram told of hearing him recite his poems. She said, "There were no indications of dissipation apparent when we saw Poe in Virginia at that time. I think he had not been drinking for a long time."

On September 24th, Edgar returned to Richmond, lectured again, and, as always, concluded with a recitation of *The Raven*. The next evening, at the home of his friends, the Talleys, he told of a letter he had received from Rufus Griswold. Edgar explained that he had asked Griswold to be his literary executor, in case of death, and that the letter contained Griswold's agreement to accept the responsibility.

From the moment of his leaving Richmond, possibly on September 27th, Edgar's exact movements have never been traced. He announced his plans to take the boat to Baltimore. To Elmira, who had last seen him, he appeared to be ill with a fever. In Baltimore, on October 3, 1849, Dr. James E. Snodgrass, who had known and treated Edgar previously, received a pencil note: "There is a gentleman, rather the worse for wear, at Ryan's 4th ward polls, who goes under the cognomen of Edgar A. Poe, and who appears in great distress, & he says he is acquainted with you, and I assure you, he is in need of immediate assistance." The note was signed by Joseph W. Walker, a printer on the *Baltimore Sun.*

Dr. Snodgrass hurried to the polling place at Number 44 East Lombard Street, where he found Edgar seated in an armchair in the barroom. It was evident that he was critically ill. The question of how he had arrived at the polling place has led to much conjecture. One theory is that, because of the election that was being held in Baltimore, Edgar had fallen into the hands of men who had drugged him, or plied him with liquor, and then led him to various polling places, where he was forced to vote again and again as a "repeater."

His clothes had been stolen, and, according to Dr. Snodgrass, he was dressed in a "sack-coat of thin and sleezy black alpaca, ripped more or less at intervals of its seams, and faded and soiled, and pants of a steel-mixed pattern of cassinett, half worn and badly fitting, if they could be said to fit at all. . . ." In his hand he held a cane which he had taken from Dr. Carter in Richmond.

Edgar was carried to the Washington College Hospital on Wednesday, October 3rd. He had a short period of consciousness the next morning. His attending physician, Dr. J. J. Moran, tried to talk to him and to find out what had happened, but Edgar's answers were incoherent. For the next three days he alternated between periods of delirium and short moments of rationality.

During the night of Saturday, October 6th, recollections of the past and of his first writings may have possessed his fevered mind. Perhaps he was thinking of the sea and of the terrifying scenes he had created in *Arthur Gordon Pym;* for he began suddenly to shout, "Reynolds! Reynolds!" It was a strange return to the past, for Jeremiah Reynolds was the man whose accounts of voyages had fascinated Edgar.

Early on Sunday morning, October 7th, Edgar lay calm and quiet, as though he had passed through the stormy seas and reached the end of his voyage safely. He moved his head slightly and murmured, "Lord help my poor soul." Seconds later he was dead.

A eulogy for Edgar Allan Poe can be drawn from only one source—his own words and thoughts. In his Preface to *The Raven* he wrote, *"With me poetry has not been a purpose, but a passion; and the passions should be held in reverence."* He lived his life with passion and with passionate devotion to beauty and the purity of creation. For this the world will forever hold *him* in reverence.

Bibliography

Allen, Hervey: *Israfel: The Life and Times of Edgar Allan Poe,* New York, 1934, Rinehart and Co., 748 pp.

Bondurant, Agnes M.: *Poe's Richmond,* Richmond, Va., 1942, Garrett and Massie, 264 pp.

Harrison, James A.: *Life and Letters of Poe,* New York, 1902–1903, Thomas Y. Crowell and Co. Two volumes: Vol. 1, 453 pp.; Vol. 2, 478 pp.

Harrison, James A.: *New Glimpses of Poe,* New York, 1901, Mansfield and Co., 59 pp.

Ingram, John H.: *Poe Collection,* materials at the University of Virginia. John Carl Miller (ed.) Charlottesville, Va., 1960, University of Virginia Press, 397 pp.

Ostrom, John Ward (ed.): *The Letters of Edgar Allan Poe,* Cambridge, Mass., 1948, Harvard University Press, two volumes, 664 pp.

Poe, Edgar Allan: *Complete Works of Poe,* New York, 1911 and 1917, Houghton Mifflin Co., J. H. Whitty, 339 pp.

Poe, Edgar Allan: *The Works of Edgar Allan Poe,* New York, 1927, Walter J. Black, Inc. Hervey Allen (ed.)

Quinn, Arthur Hobson: *Edgar Allan Poe, A Critical Biography,* New York, 1941, Appleton-Century-Crofts, 804 pp.

Quinn, Arthur Hobson, and Hart, R. H.: *Edgar Allan Poe Letters and Documents in the Enoch Pratt Library,* New York, 1941.

Stanard, Mary Newton: *Edgar Allan Poe Letters till now Unpublished,* in the Valentine Museum, Richmond, Va., Philadelphia, 1925.

Weiss, Susan Archer Talley: *The Home Life of Poe,* New York, 1907, 229 pp.

Winwar, Frances: *The Haunted Palace,* New York, 1959, Harper and Brothers, 408 pp.

Woodberry, George E.: *Edgar Allan Poe,* Cambridge, Mass., 1885, Houghton Mifflin and Co., 350 pp.

Index

IRWIN PORGES was born in Maywood, Illinois, in 1909 and attended school in Chicago, where he was graduated from Lake View High School.

He began to write for his high school magazine and had poems and stories published in the *Chicago Daily Journal* and the *Chicago Evening Post* when he was only twelve years old.

He first turned to music and became a pianist, doing concert work and playing with dance bands. He still belongs to the Chicago Federation of Musicians, even though he no longer follows music as a profession.

After three and a half years with the Army Air Force in World War II, Mr. Porges moved to Los Angeles and received his bachelor's and master's degrees from the University of Southern California and the University of California at Los Angeles (UCLA), respectively.

From this time on, he has made teaching his profession, first in journalism and then as an English instructor. He is presently teaching at Los Angeles Valley College at Van Nuys, California, where his specialties are English, short story writing, and the Writers' Round Table. He sponsors the Los Angeles Valley College Writers' Club, too.

Many Brave Hearts, his first book, was published by Chilton Books in 1962.